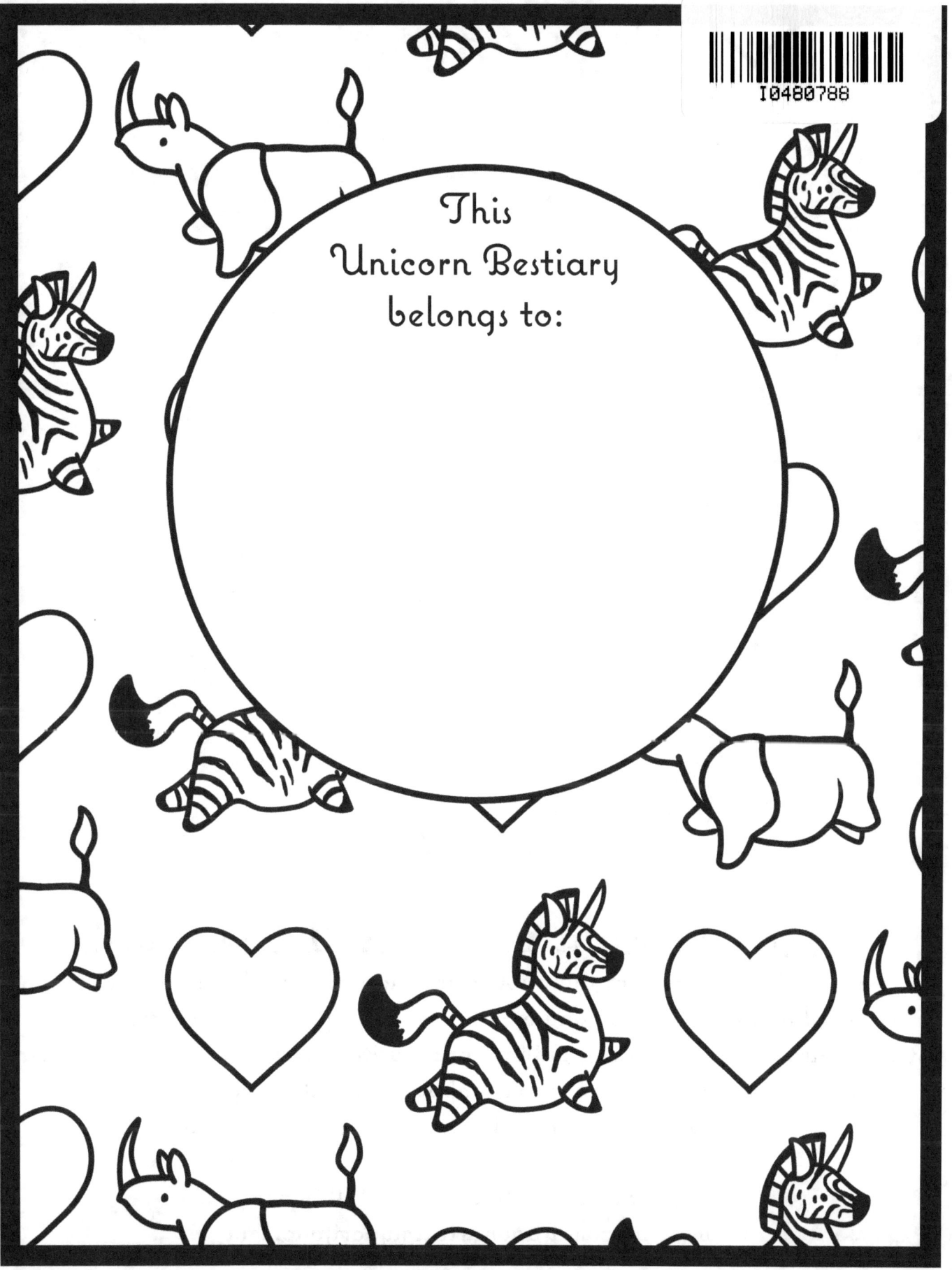

This
Unicorn Bestiary
belongs to:

Written and Illustrated by Jill Jones

www.wacomdragonartist.myportfolio.com

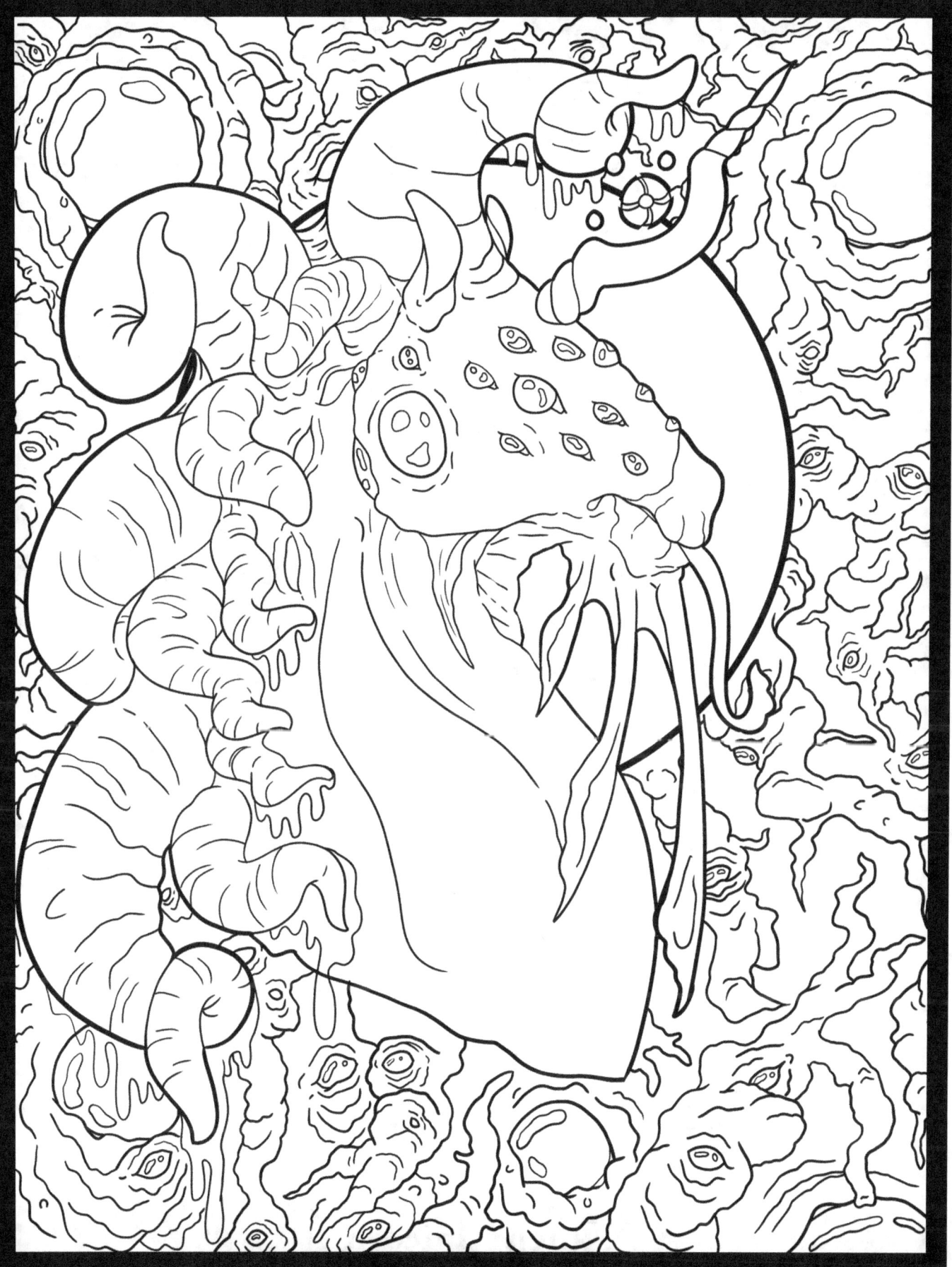

Alien Unicorn

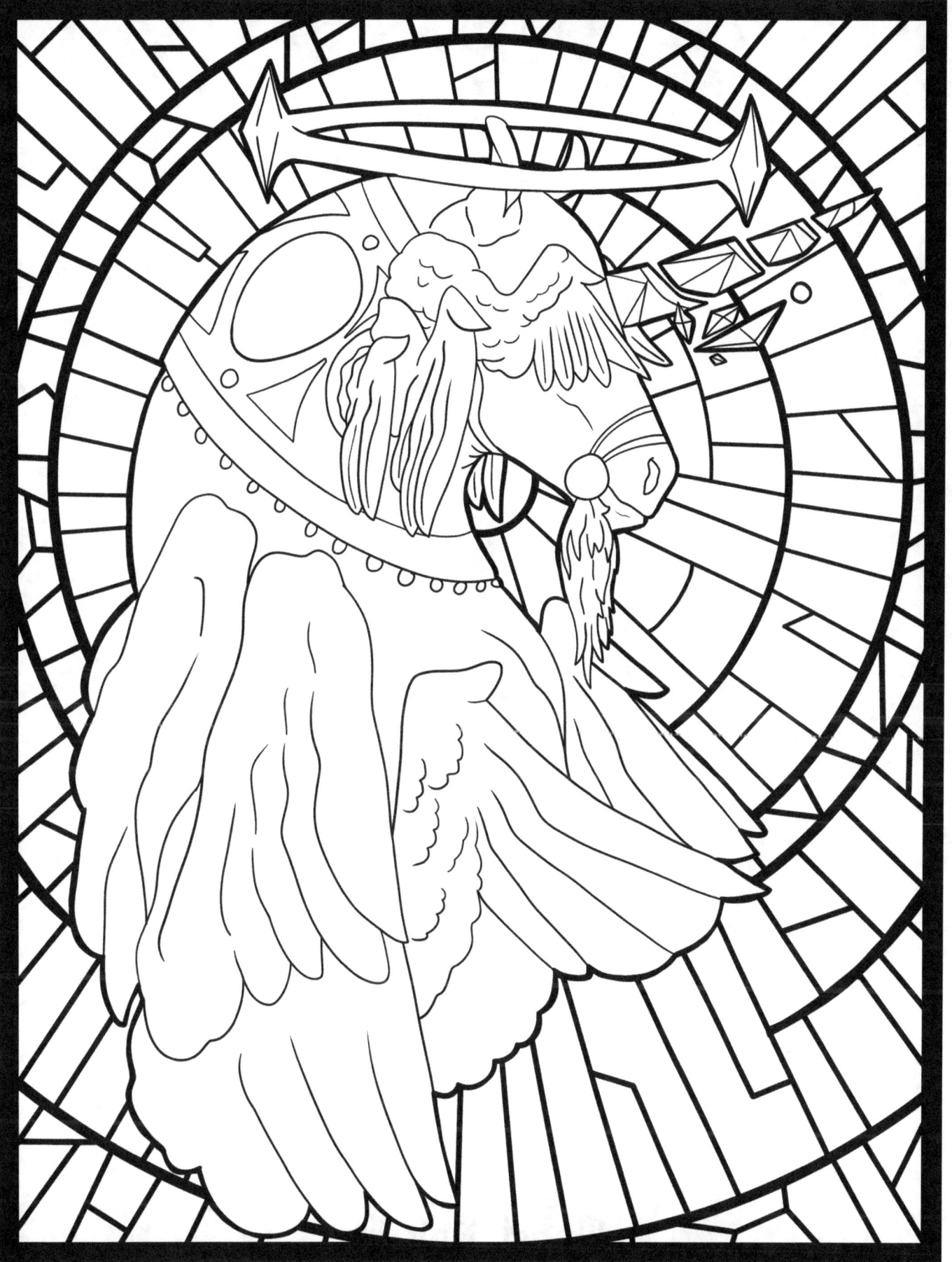

Angel Unicorn

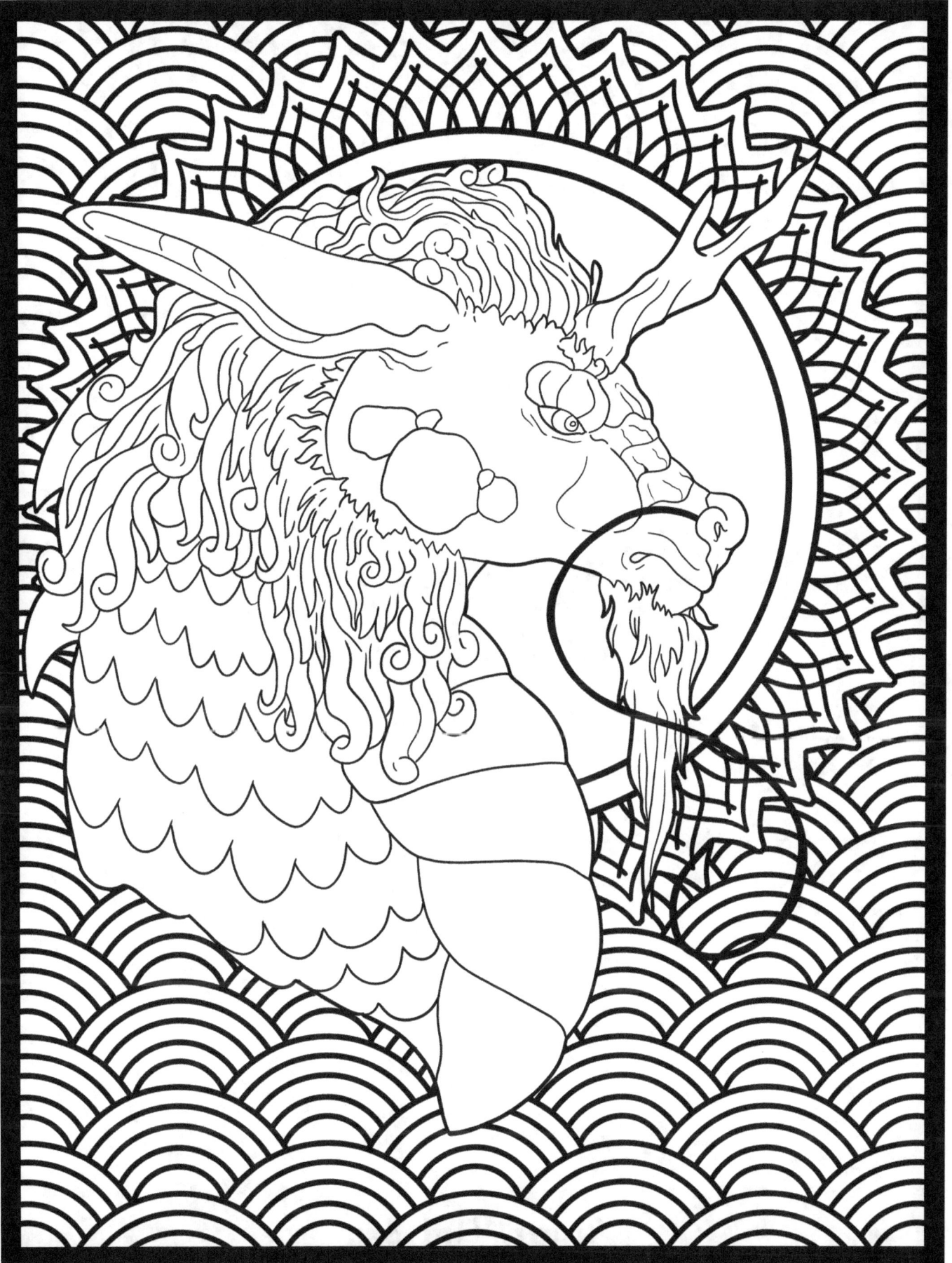

Asian Unicorn

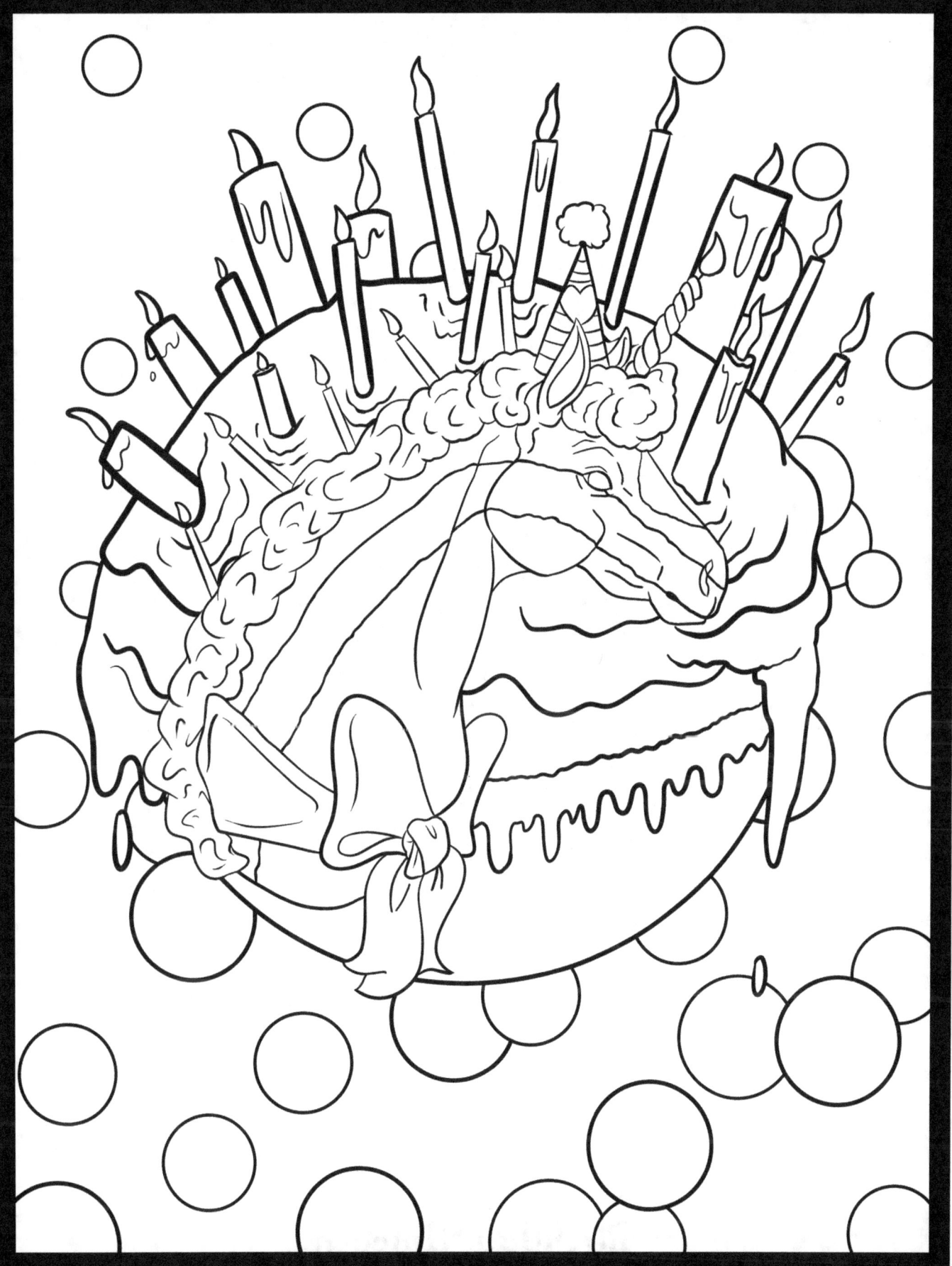

Birthday Unicorn

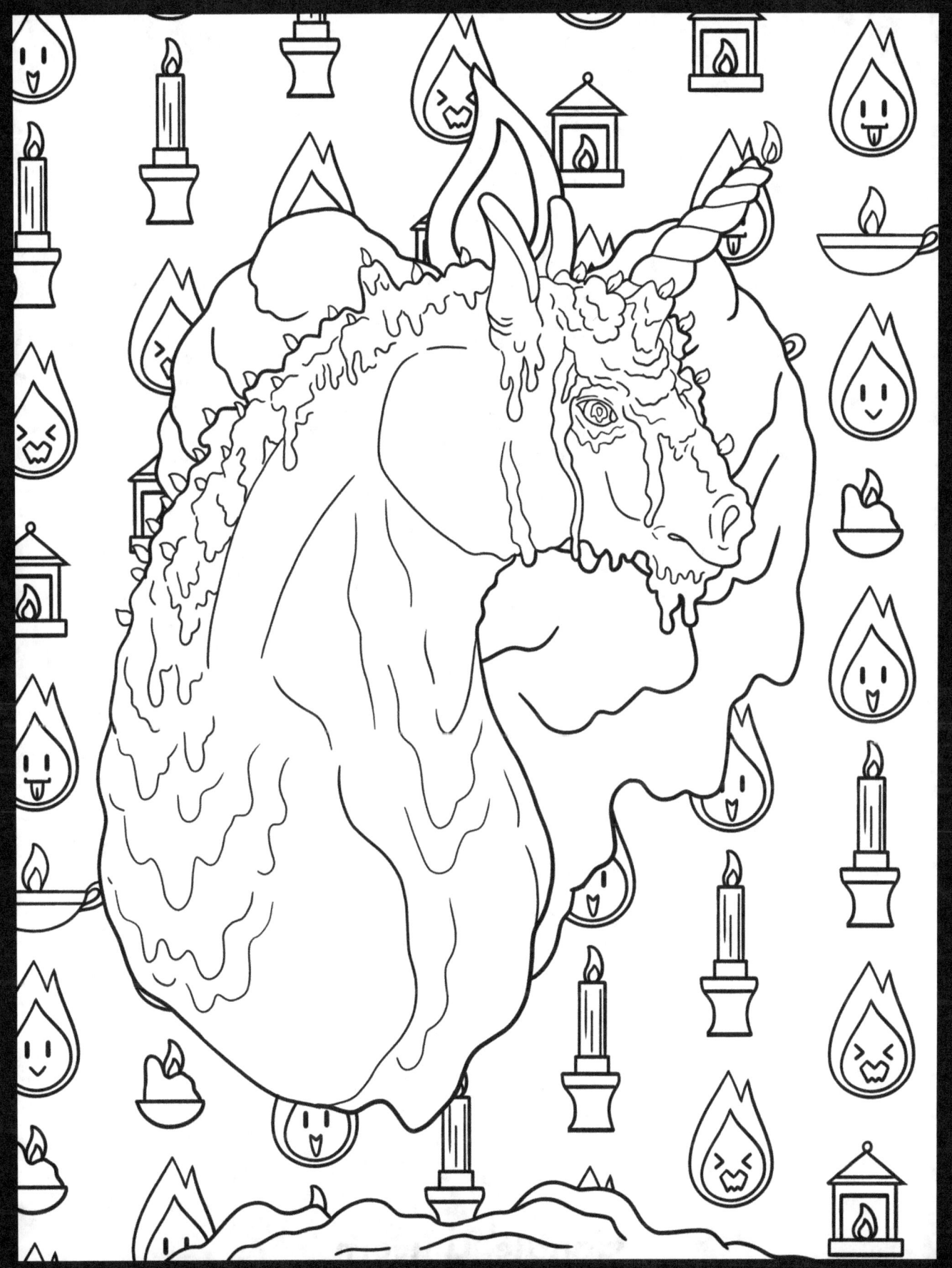

Candle Unicorn

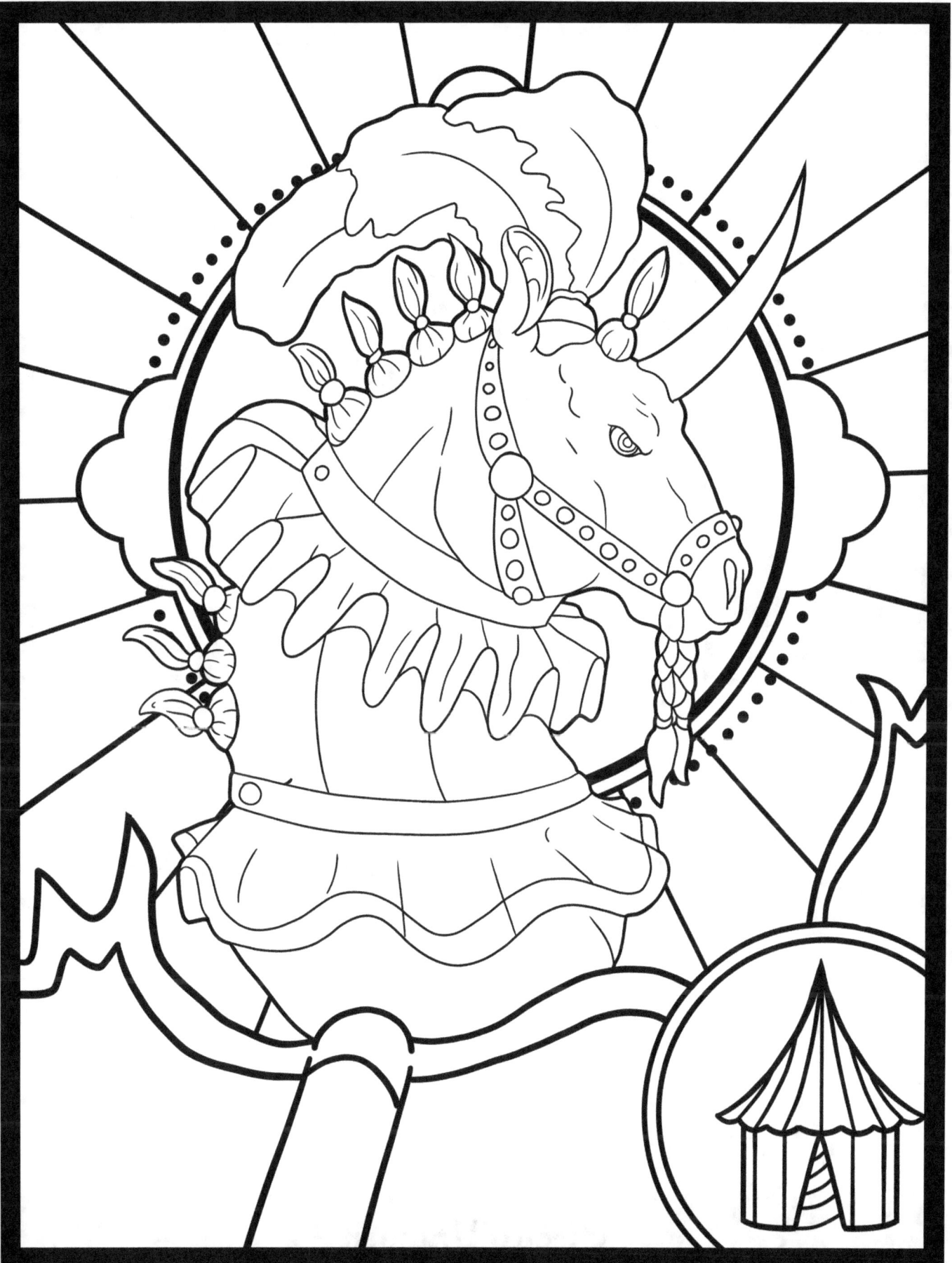

Circus Unicorn

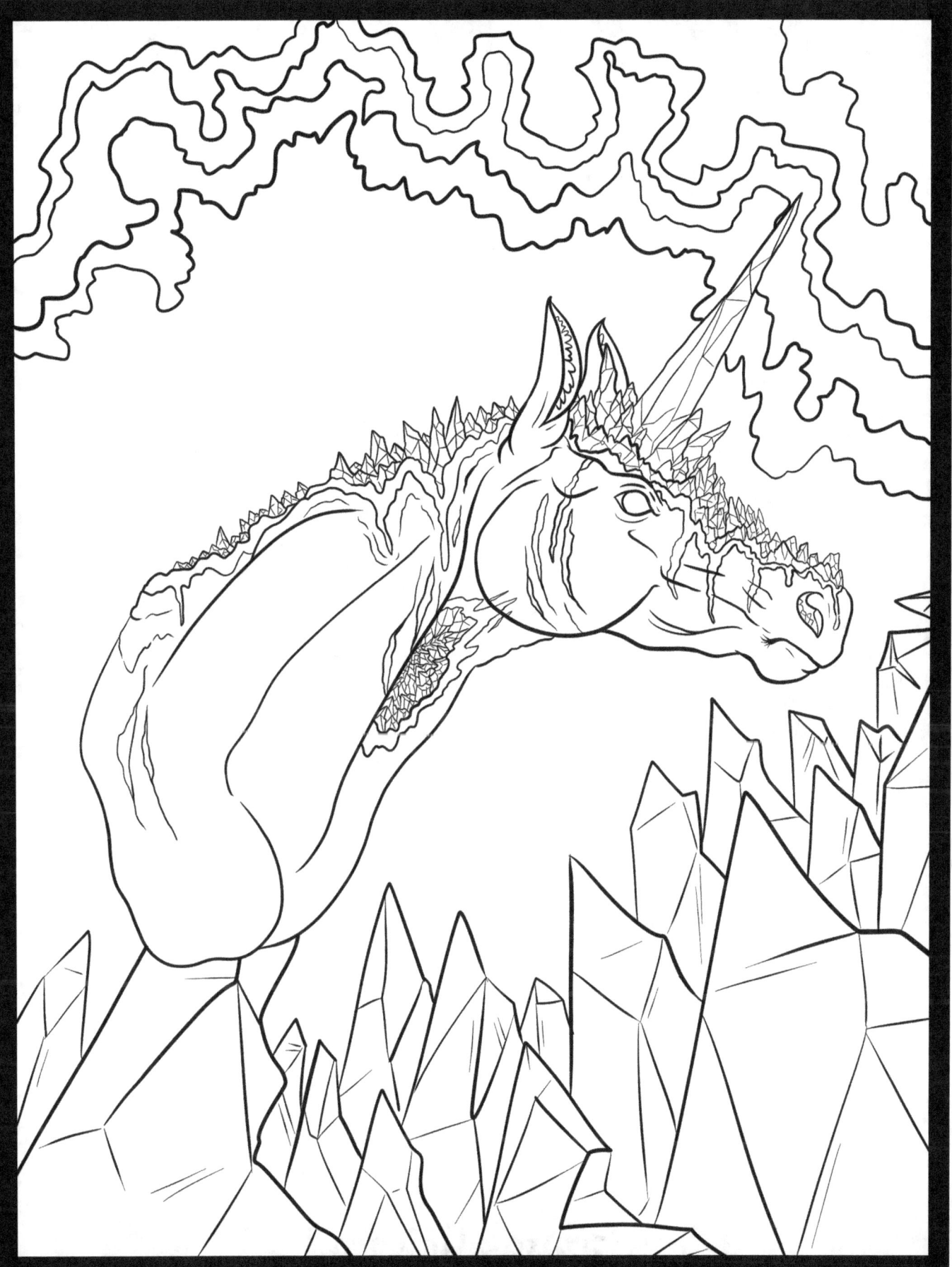

Crystal Unicorn

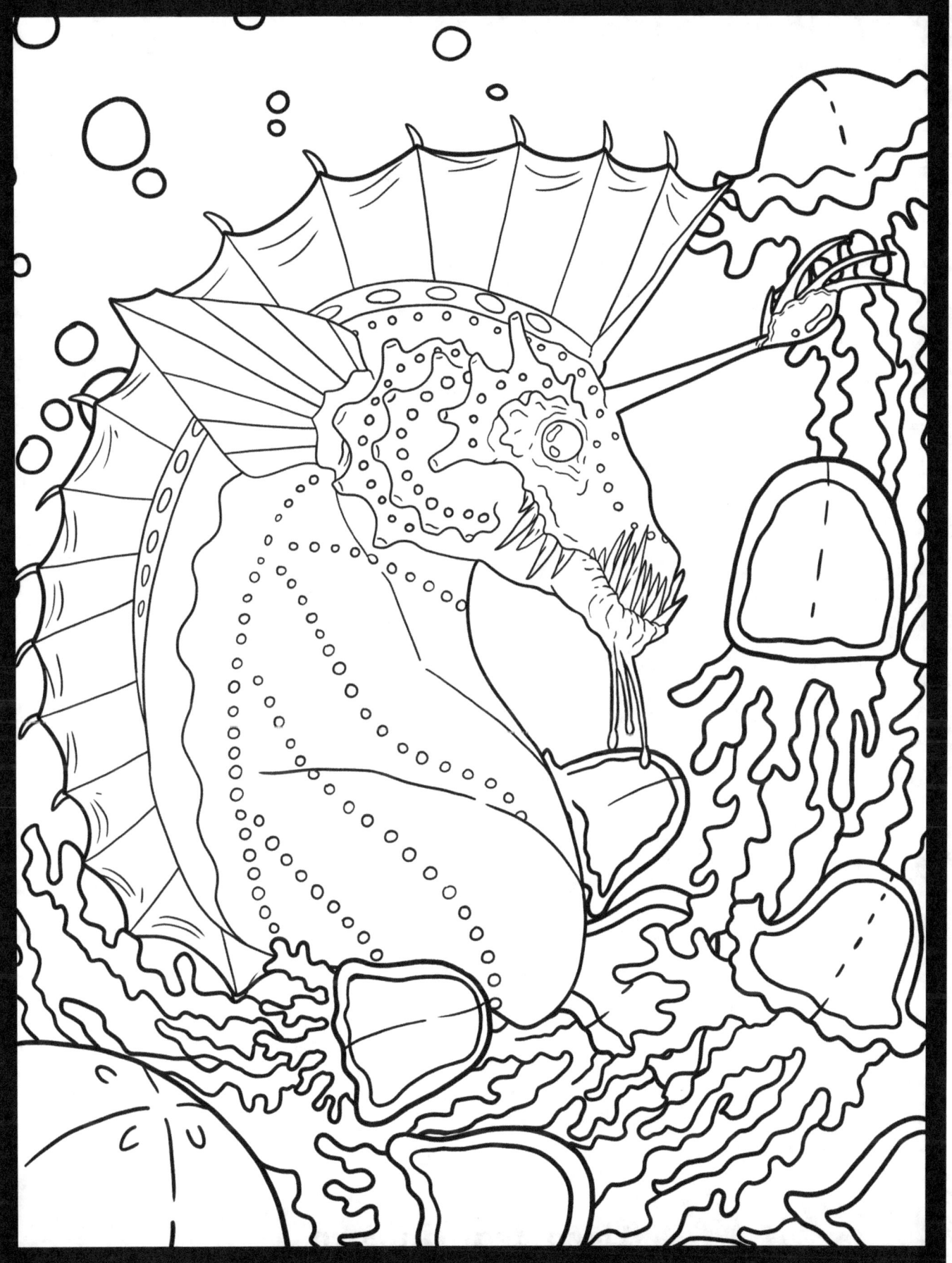

Deep Sea Unicorn

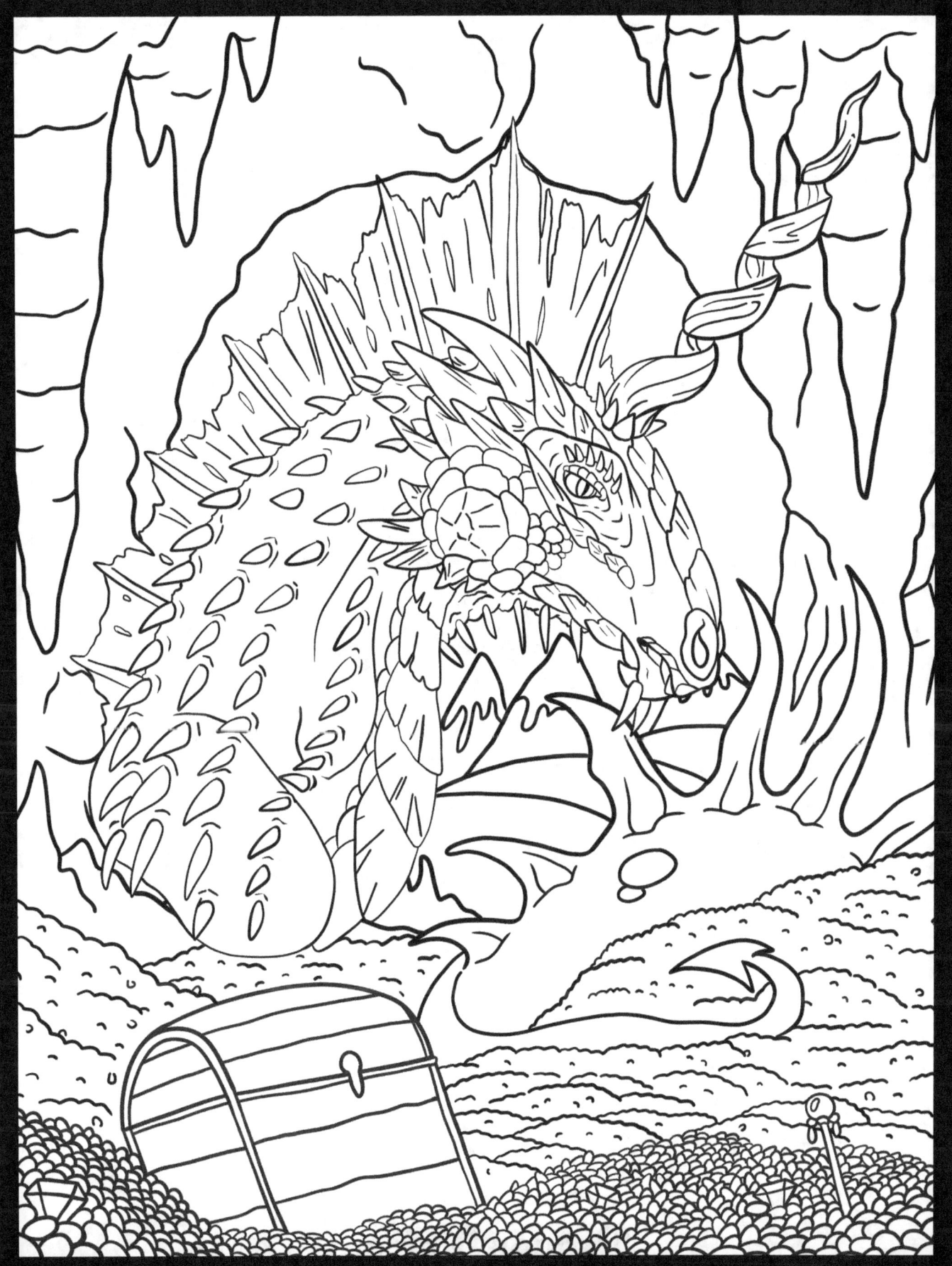

Dragon Unicorn

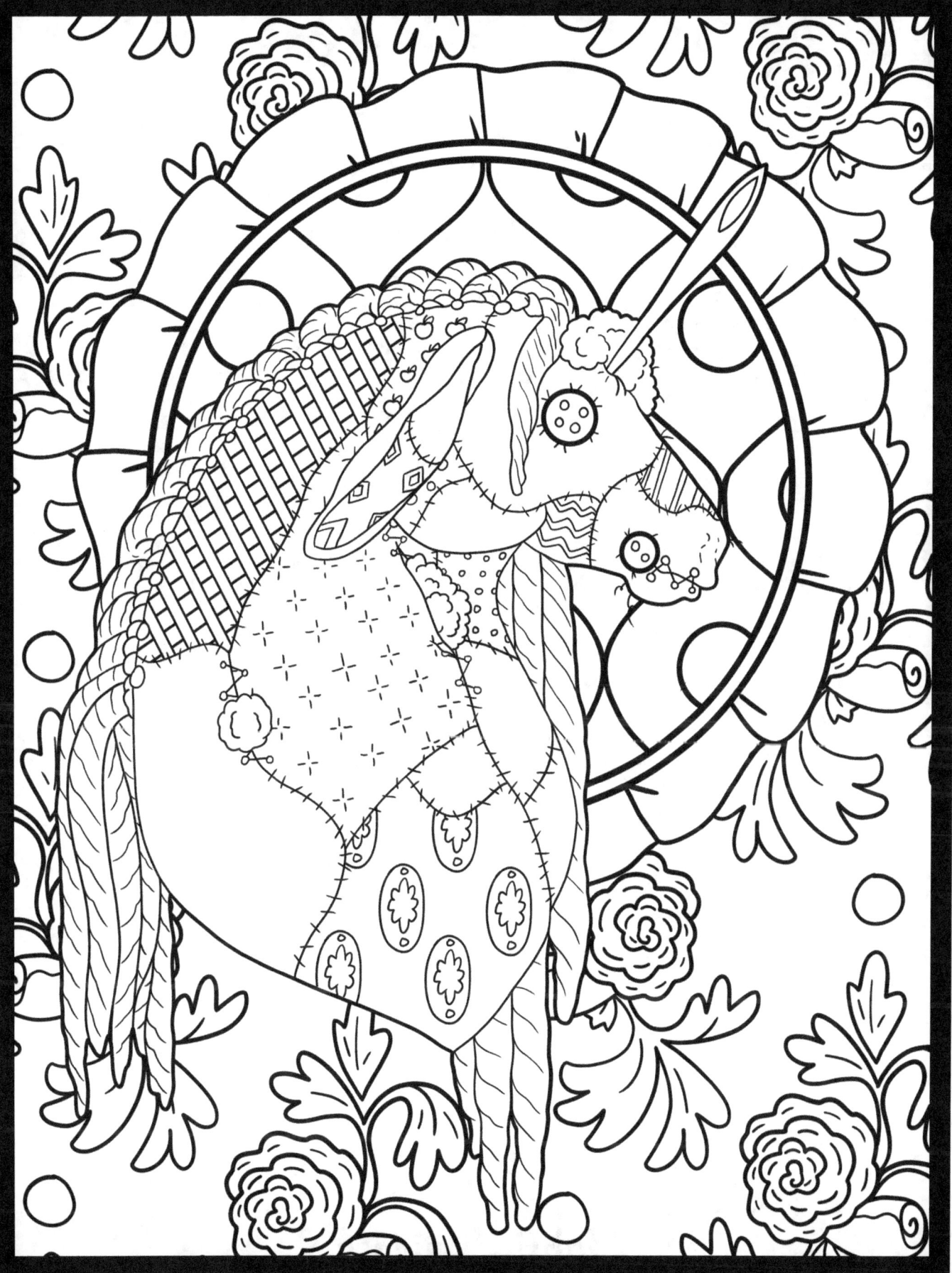

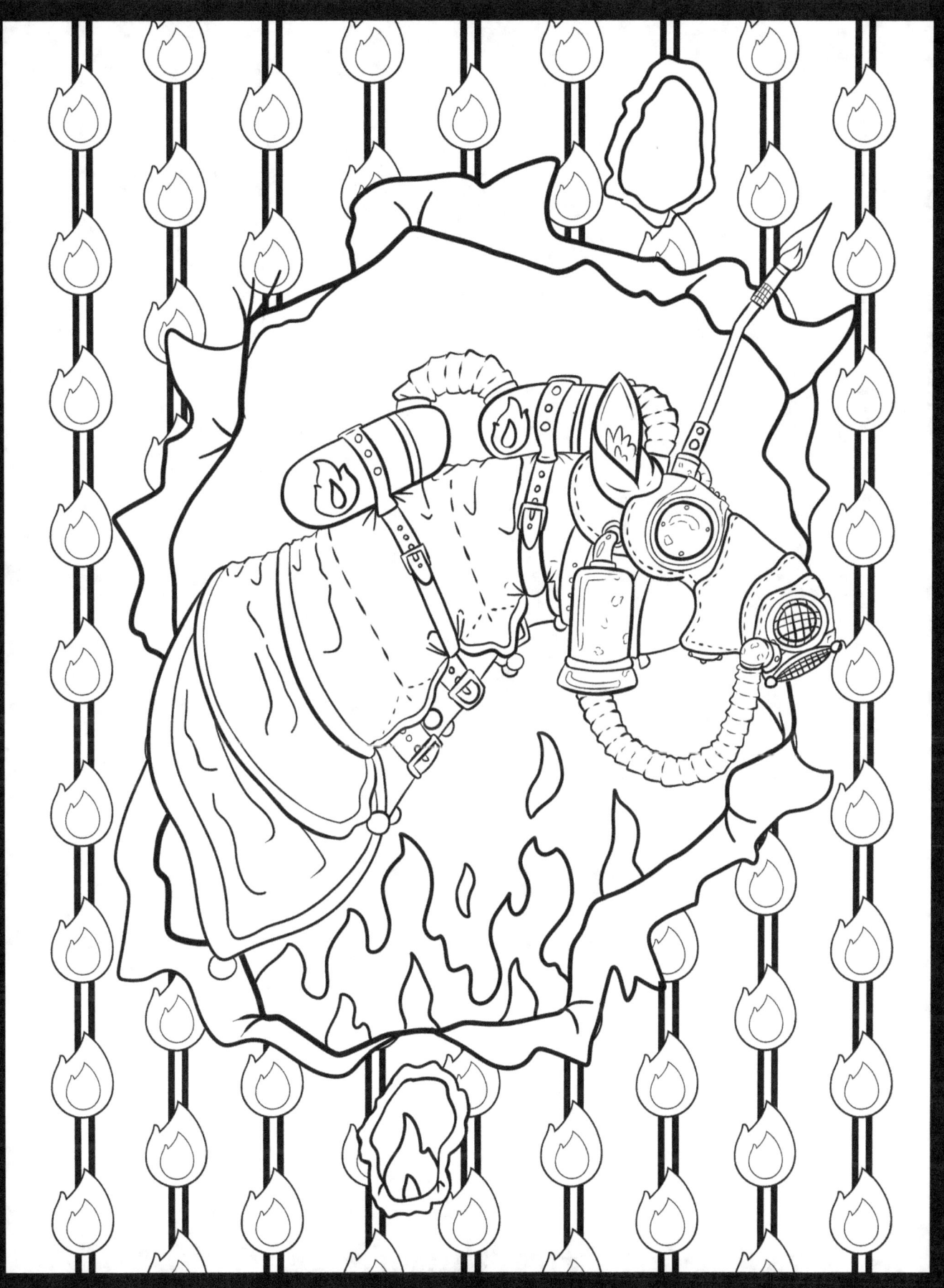

Fire Unicorn

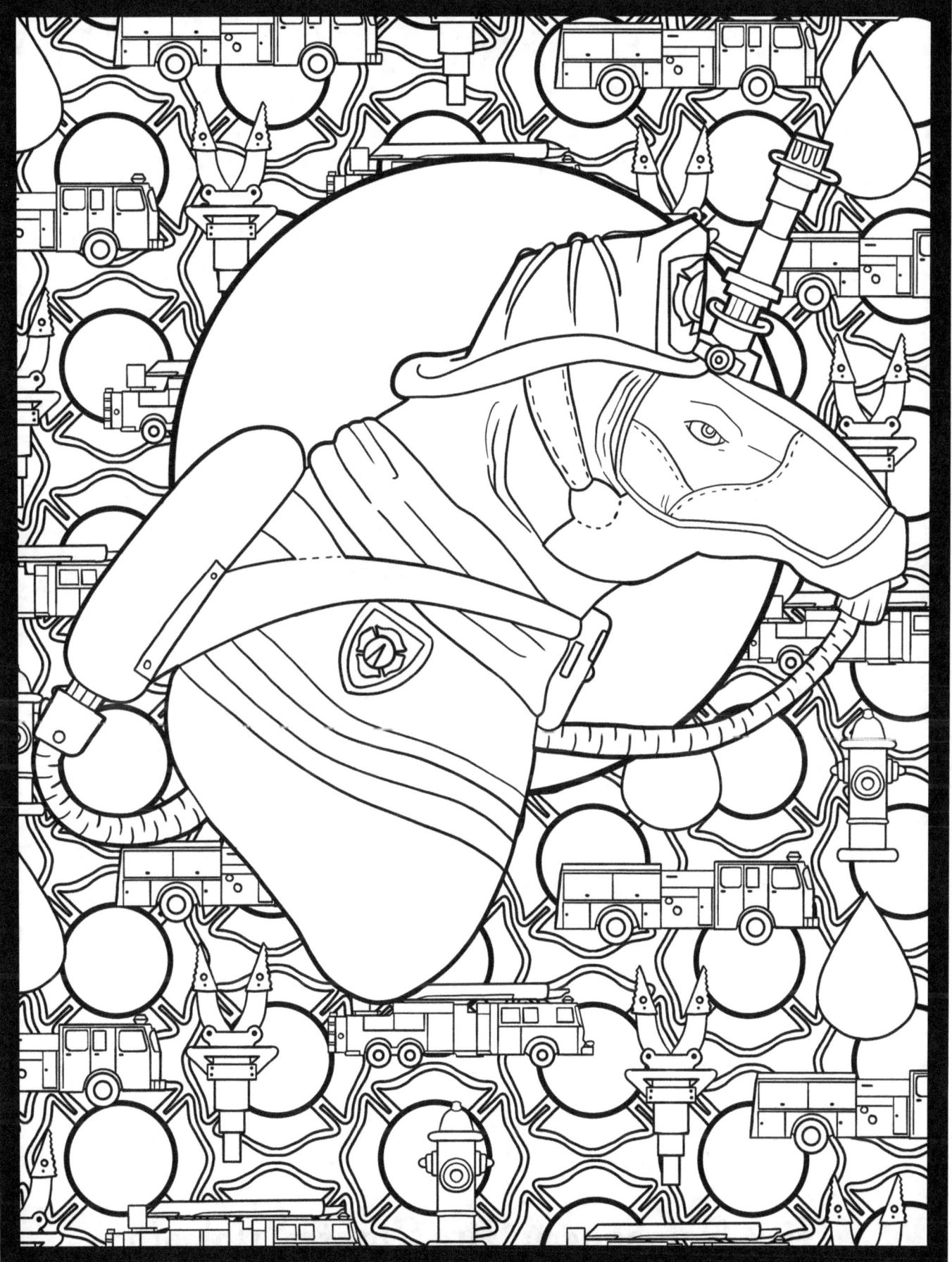

First Responders: Fire Fighter Unicorn

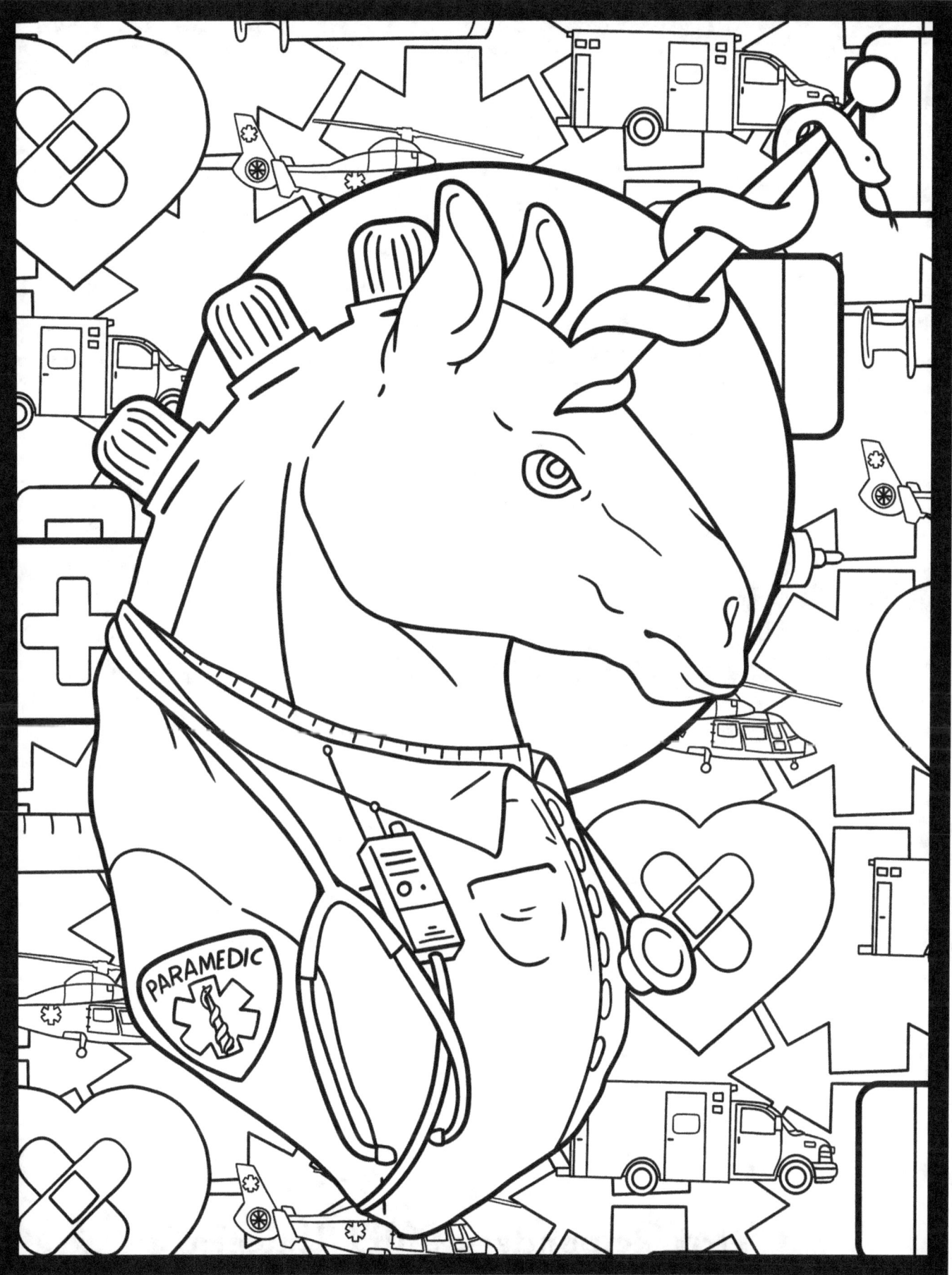

First Responders: EMS Unicorn

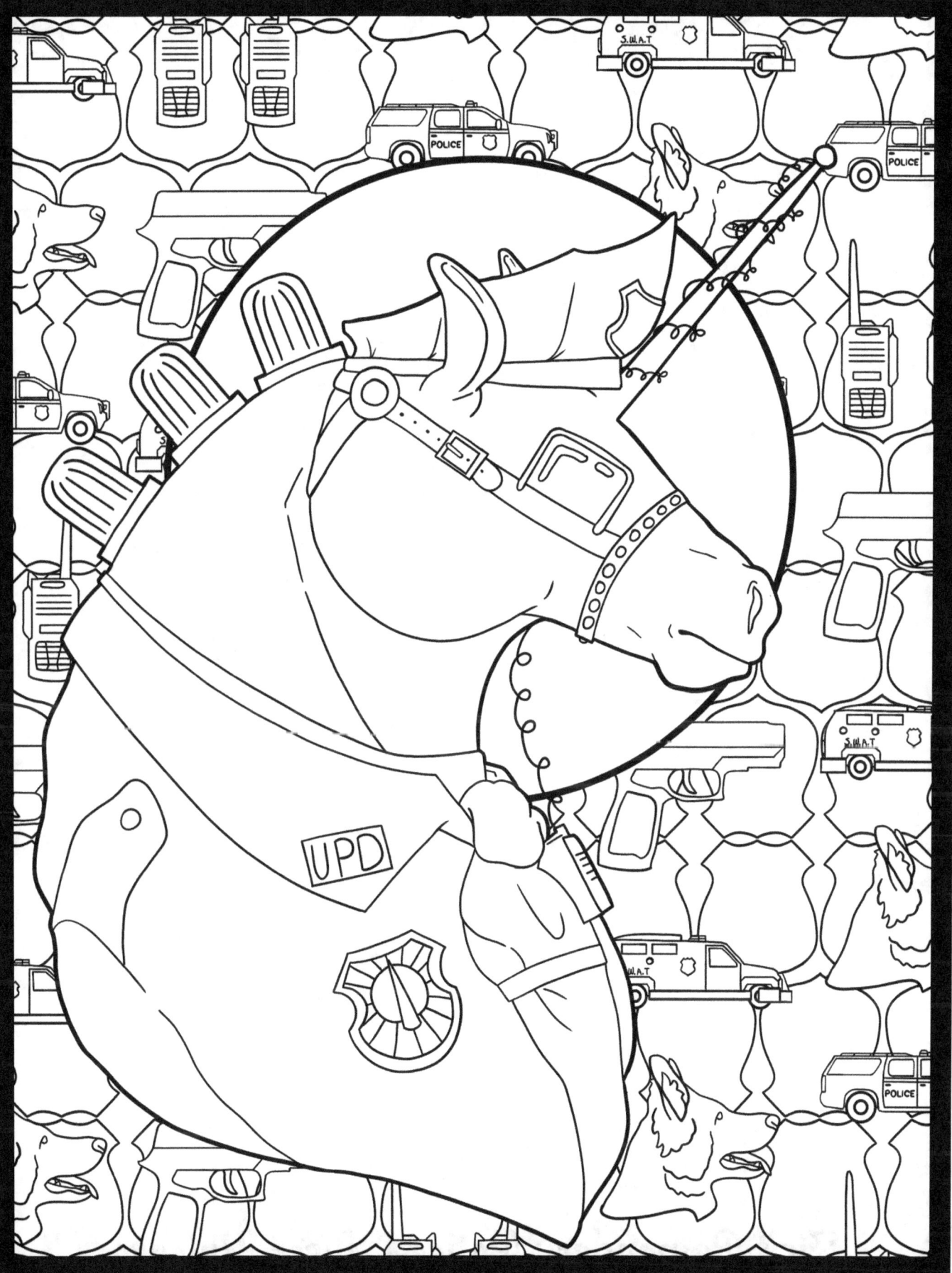

First Responders: Police Officer Unicorn

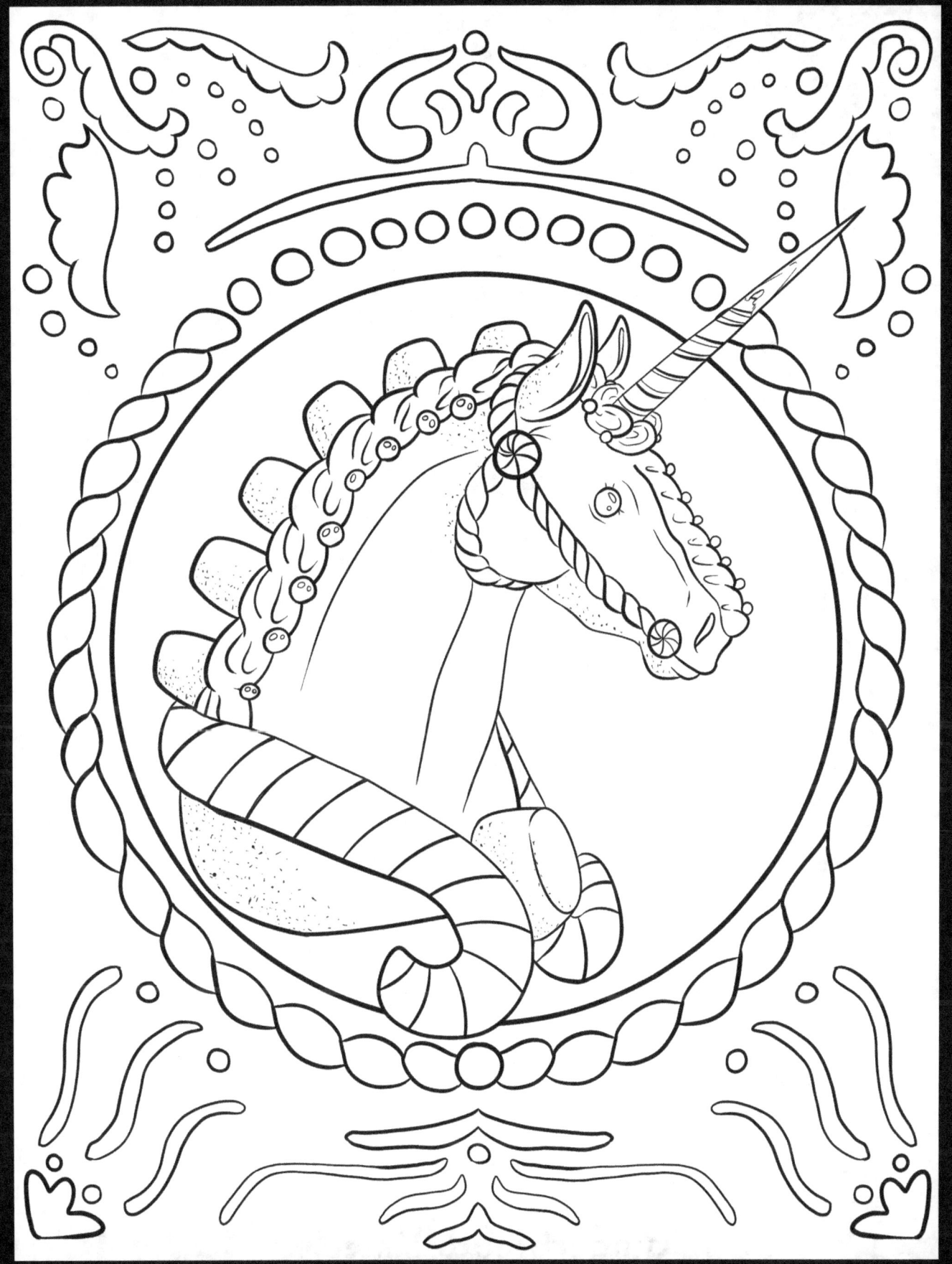

Gingerbread Unicorn

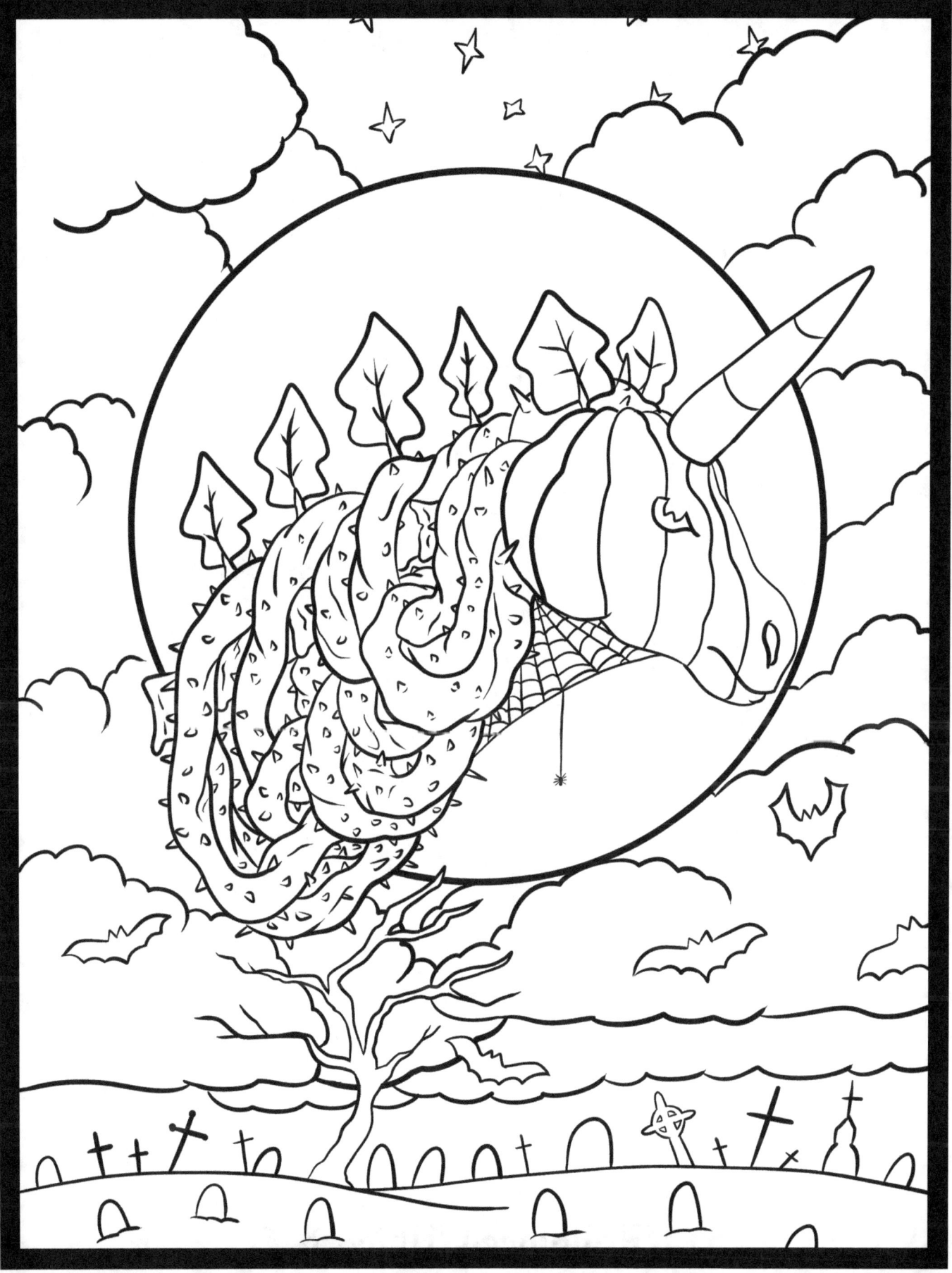

Halloween Unicorn

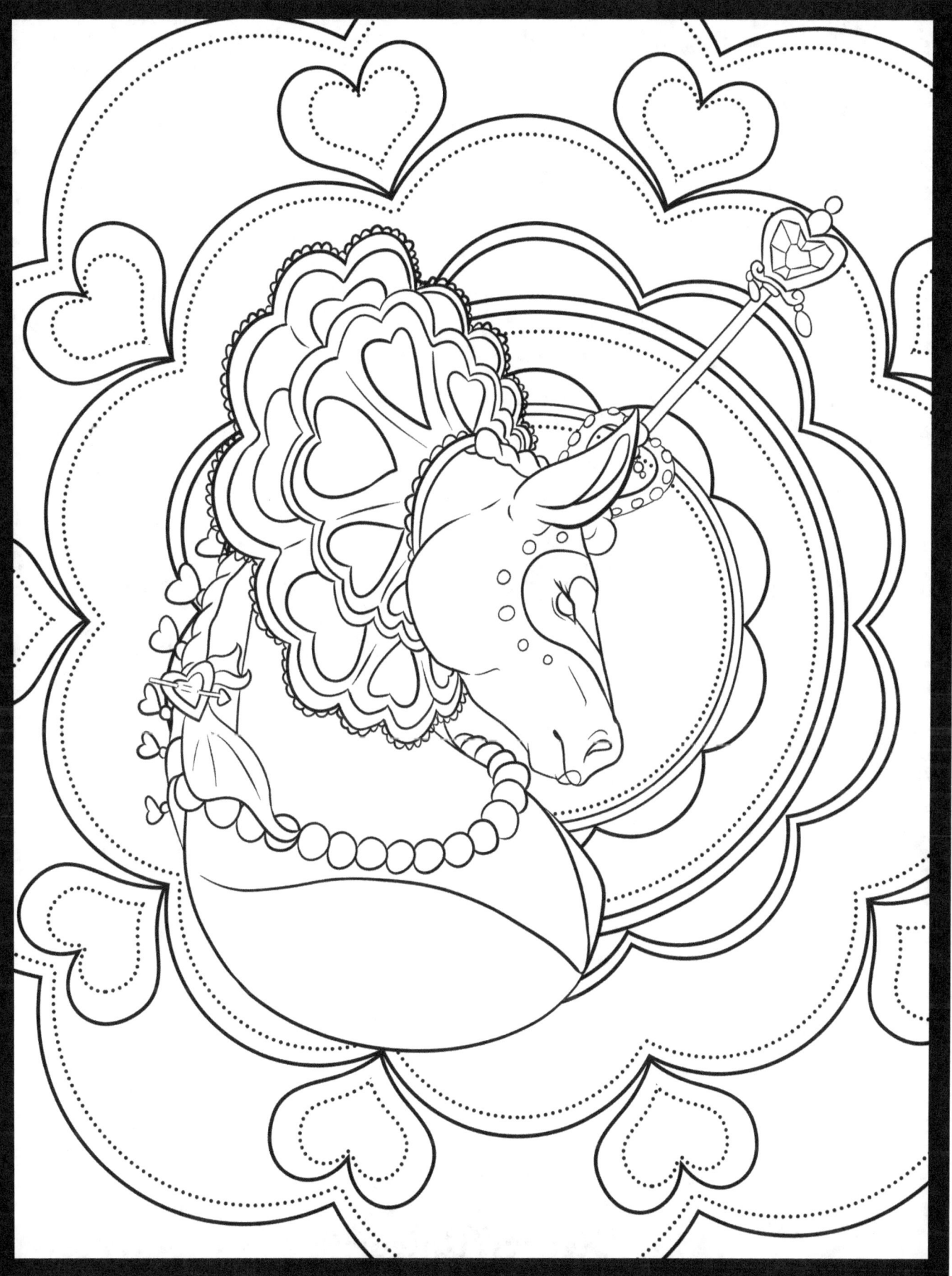

Hearts Unicorn

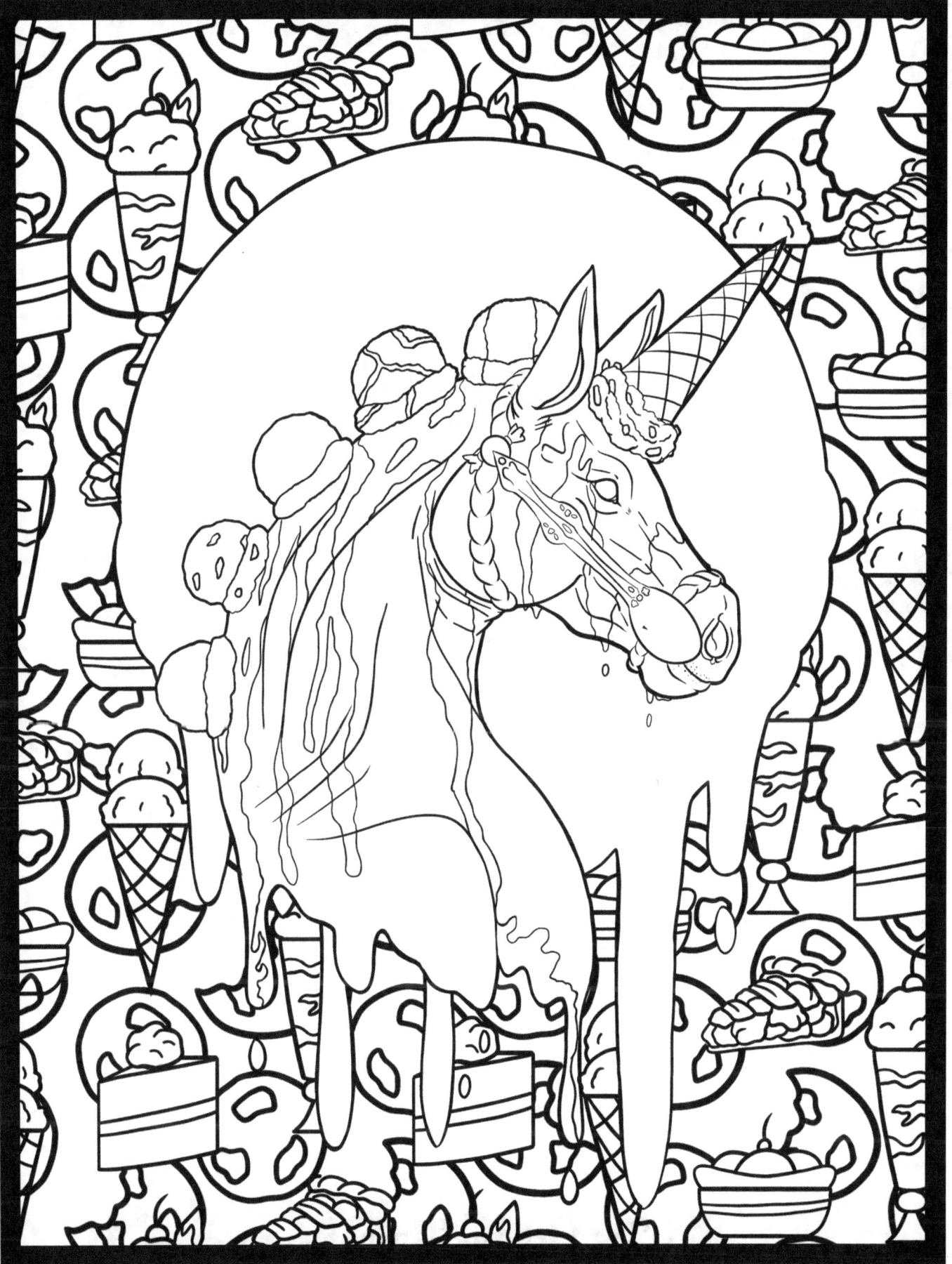

Ice Cream Unicorn

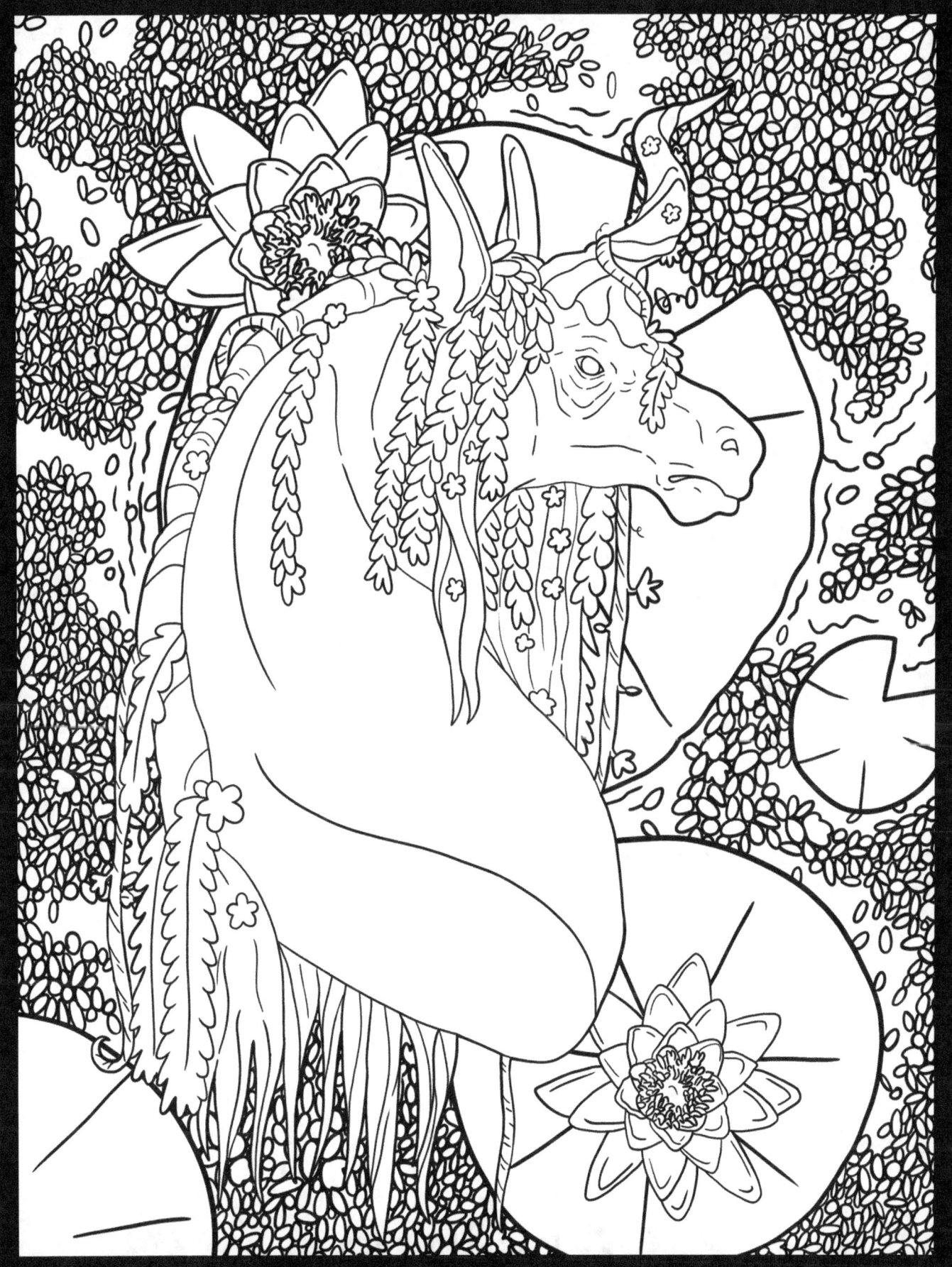

Kelpie Unicorn

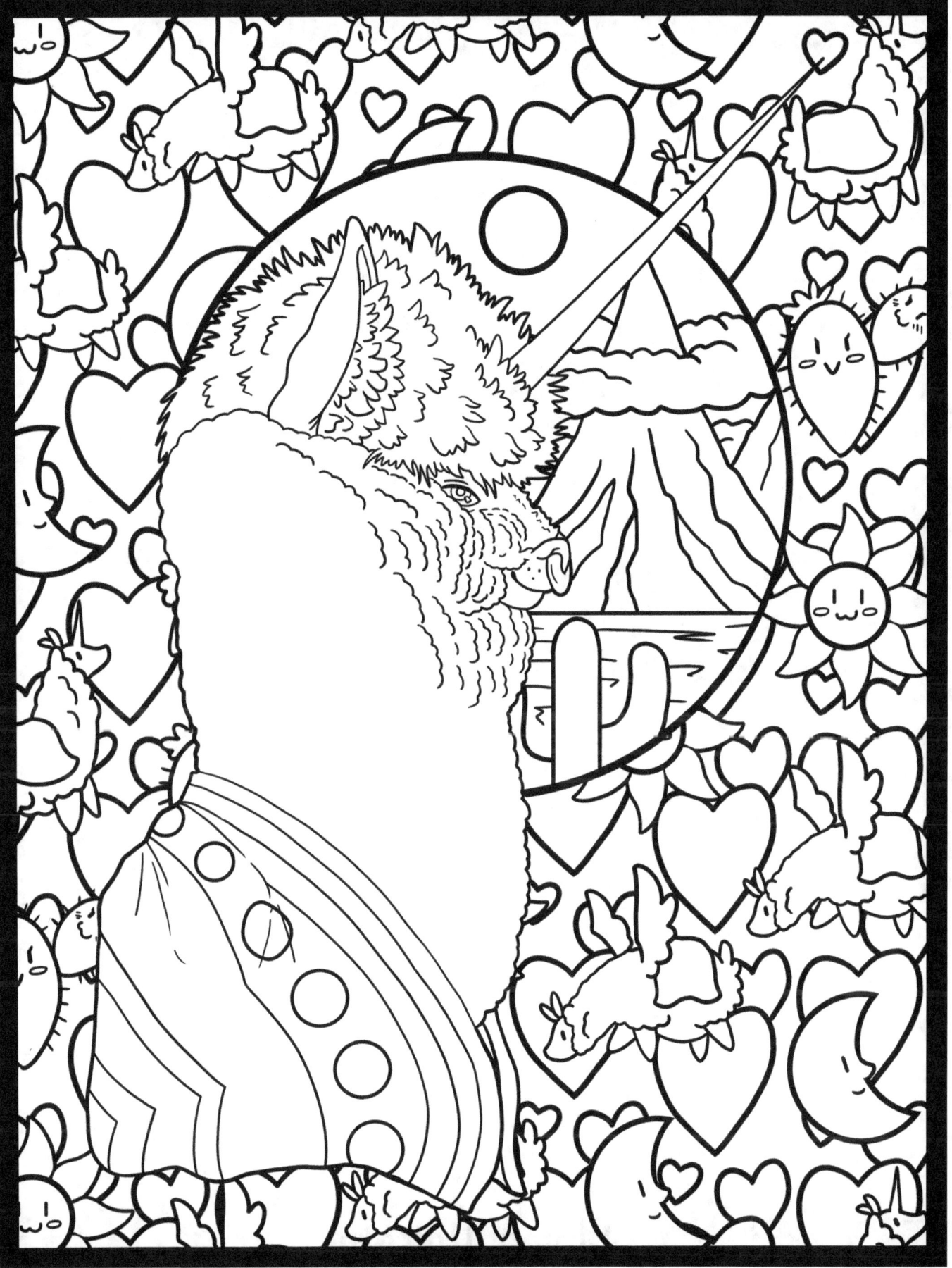

Llama Unicorn

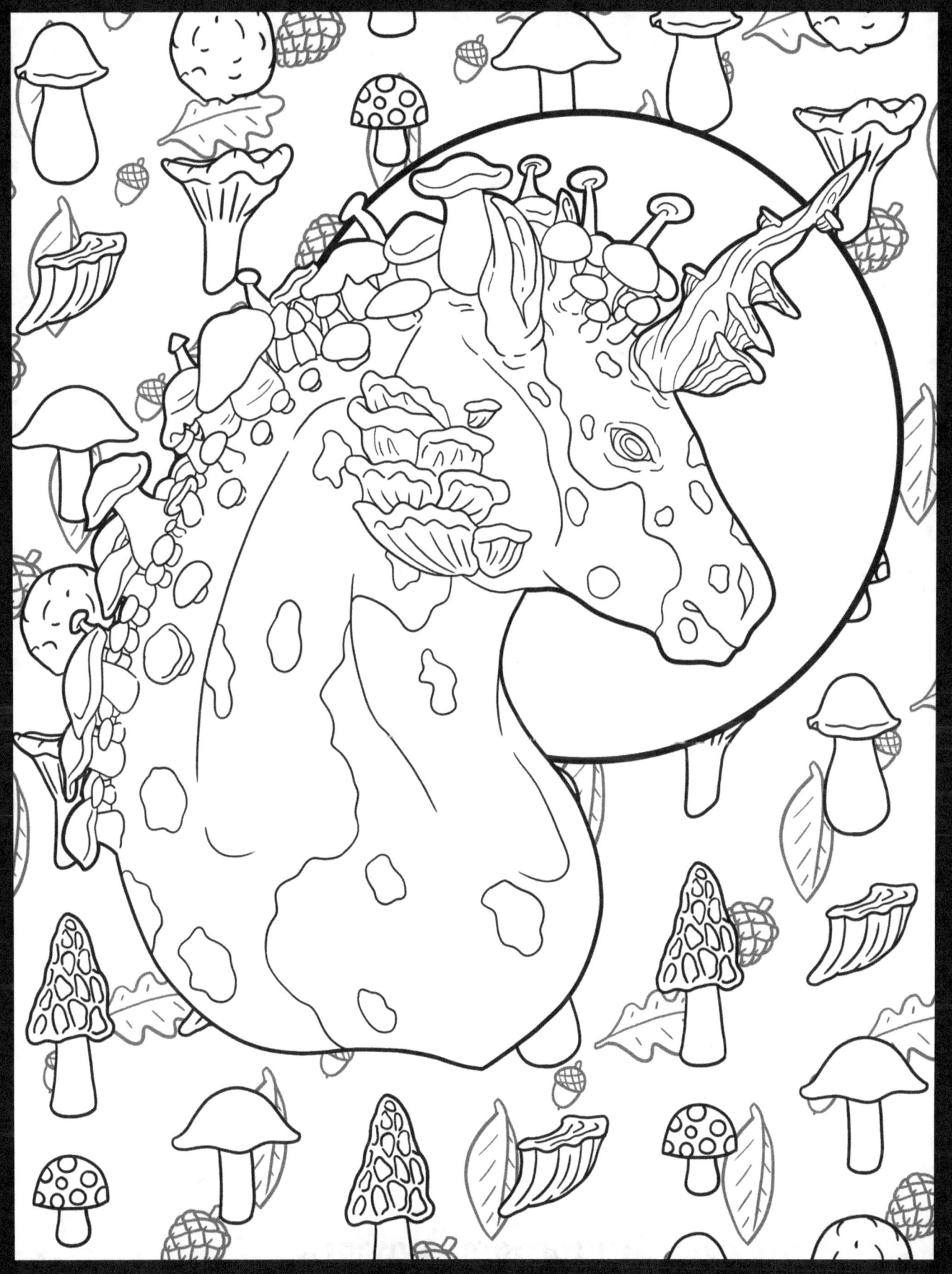

Mushroom Unicorn

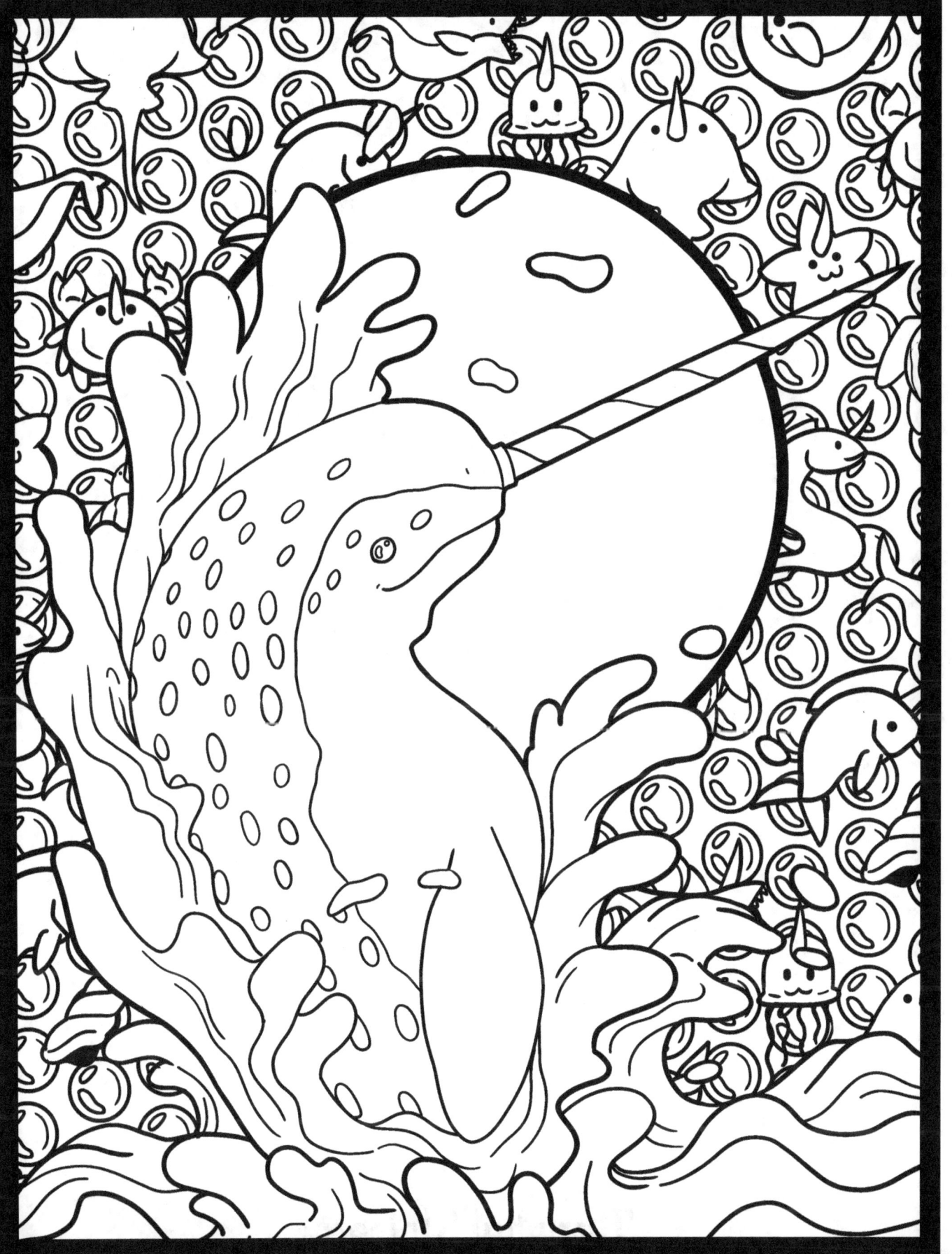

Narwhal Unicorn

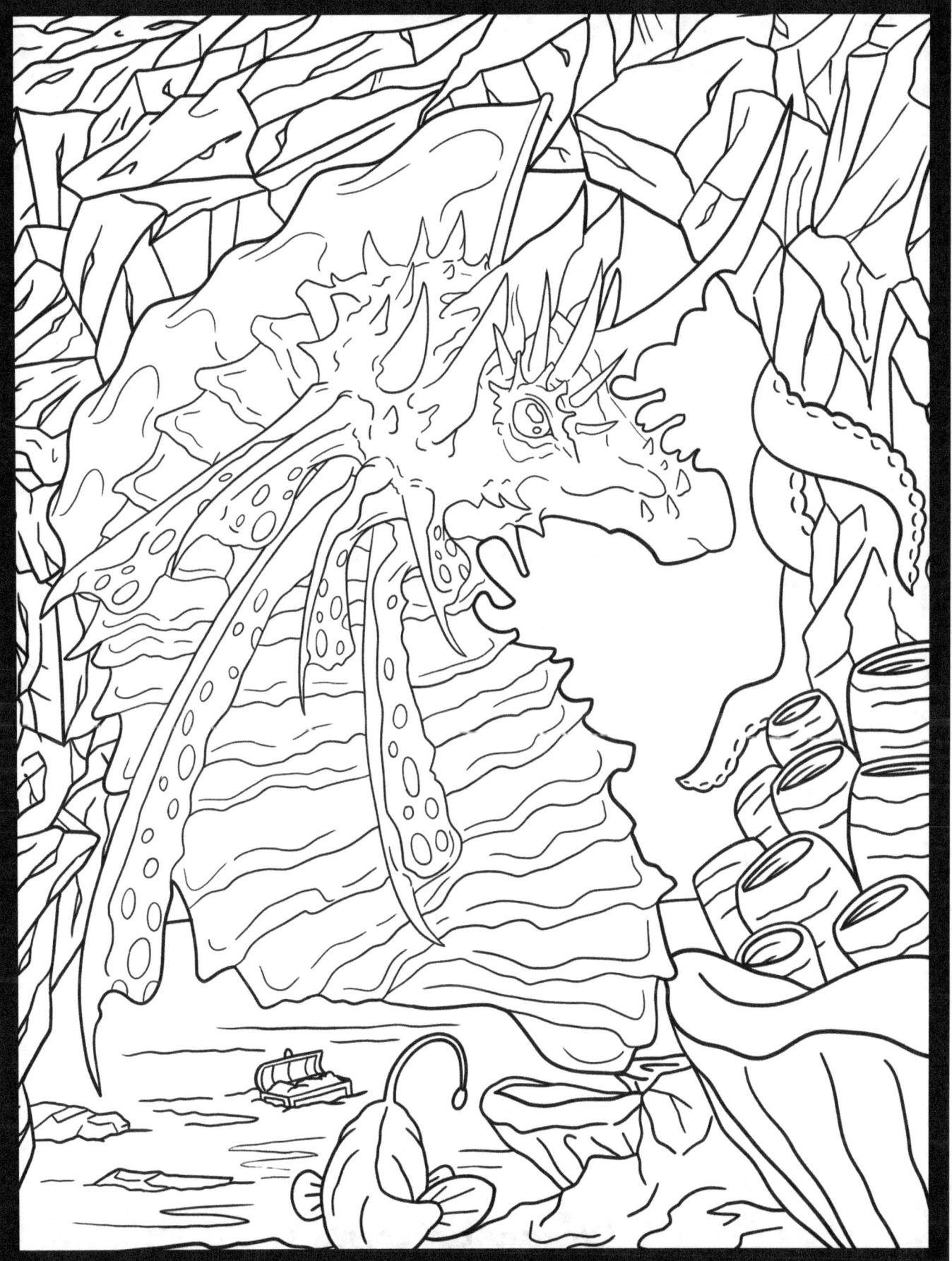

Ocean Unicorn

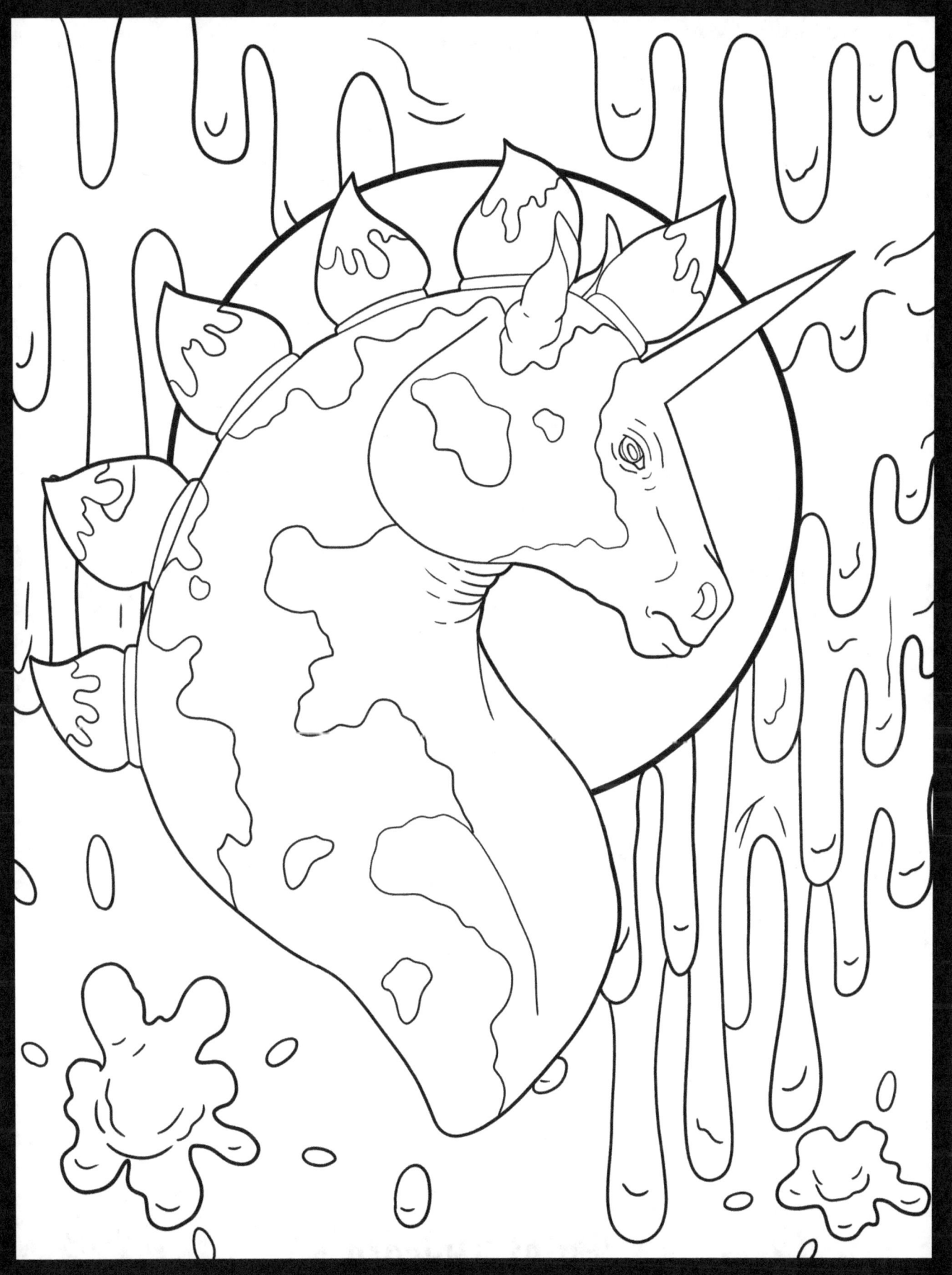

Paint Unicorn

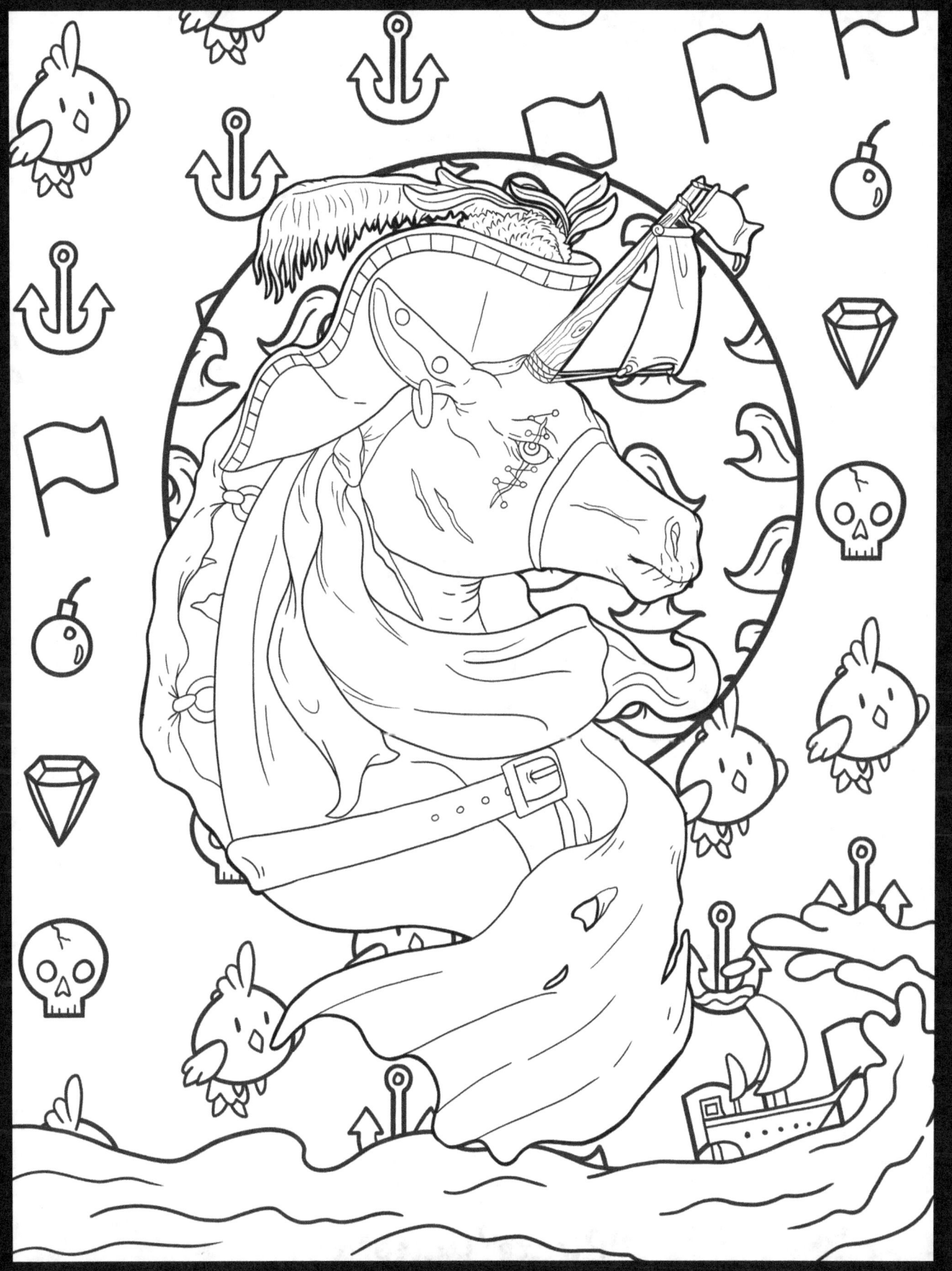

Pirate Unicorn

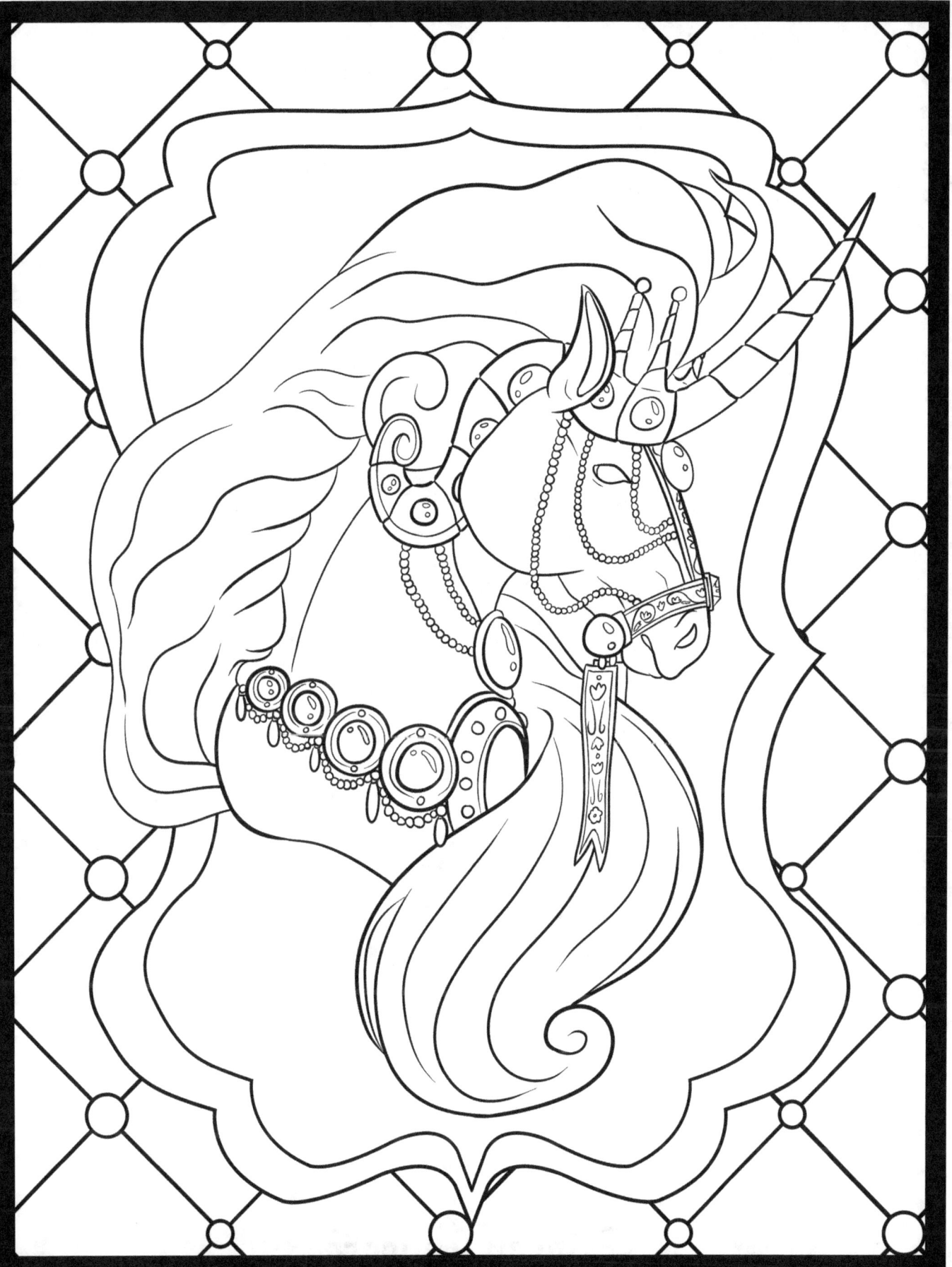

Princess Unicorn

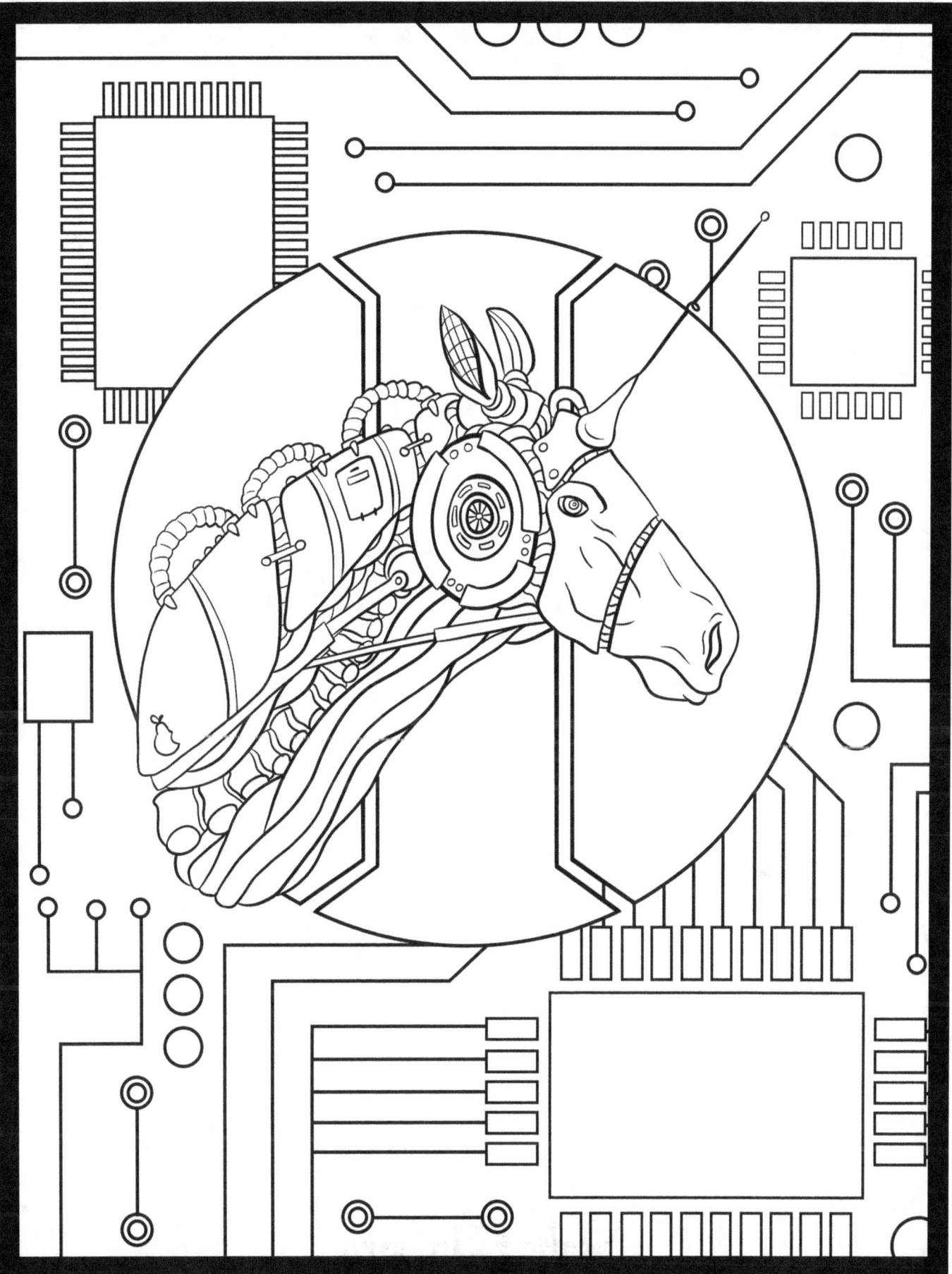

Robot Unicorn

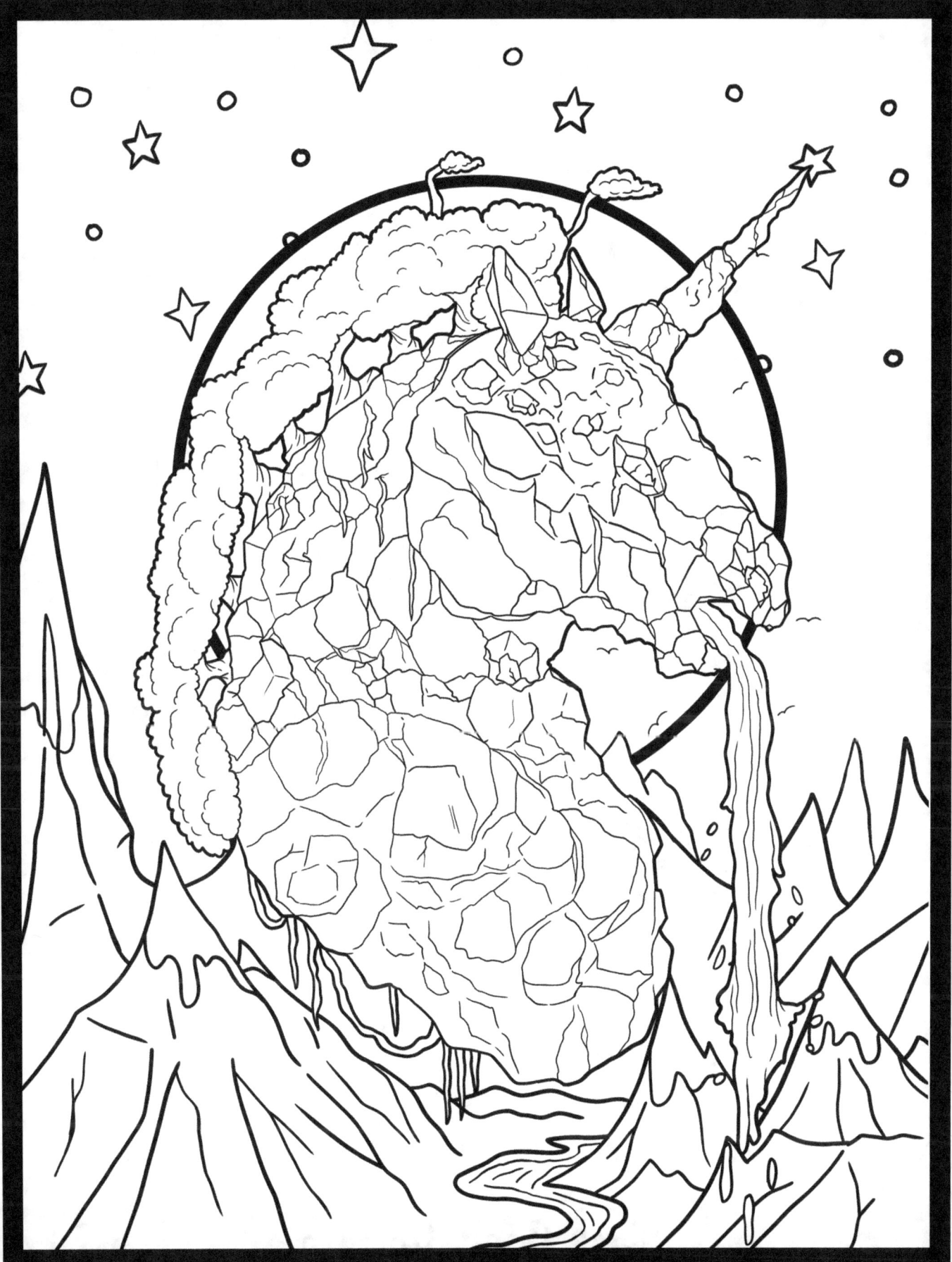

Rock Land Unicorn

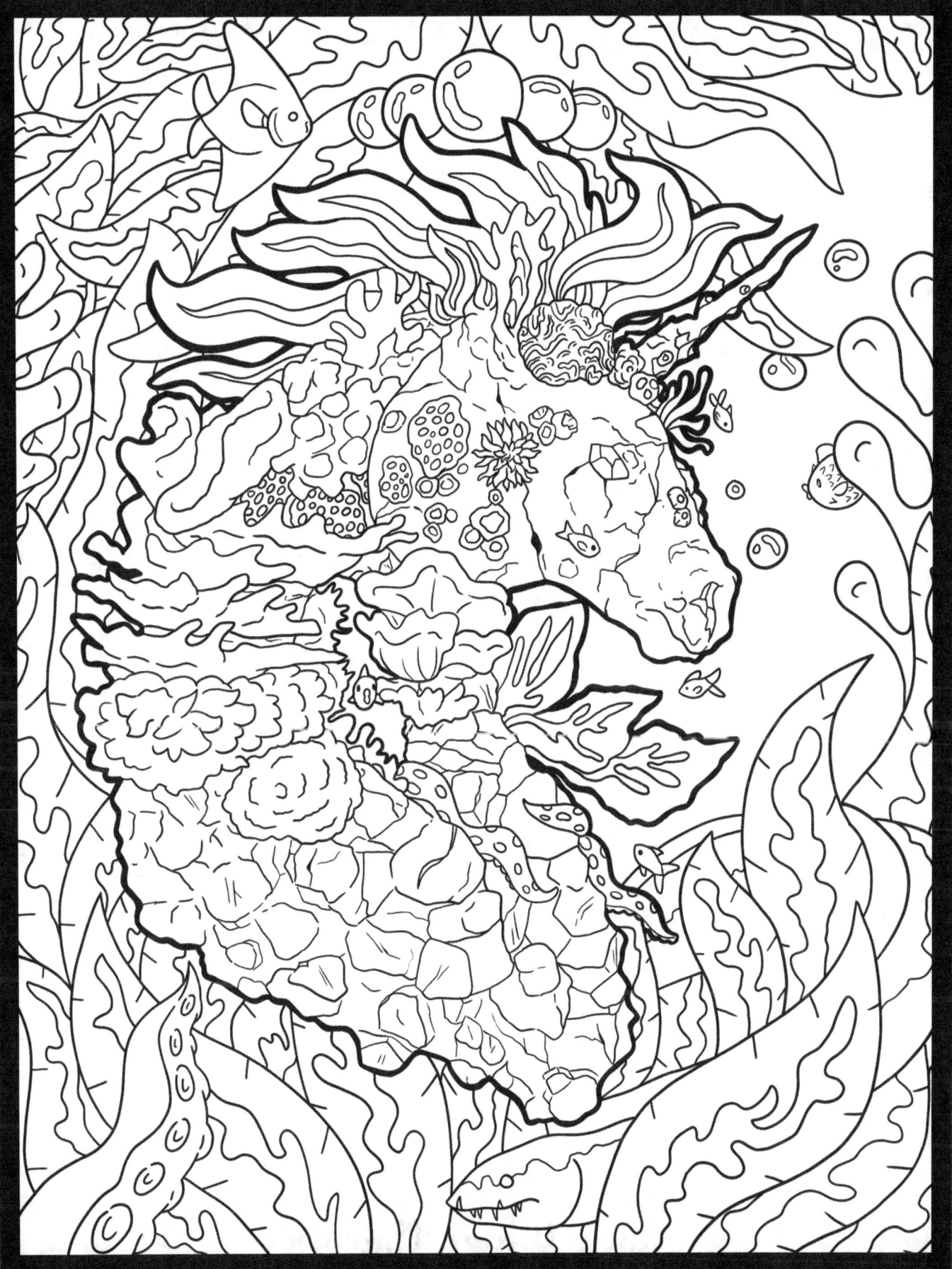

Rock Water Unicorn

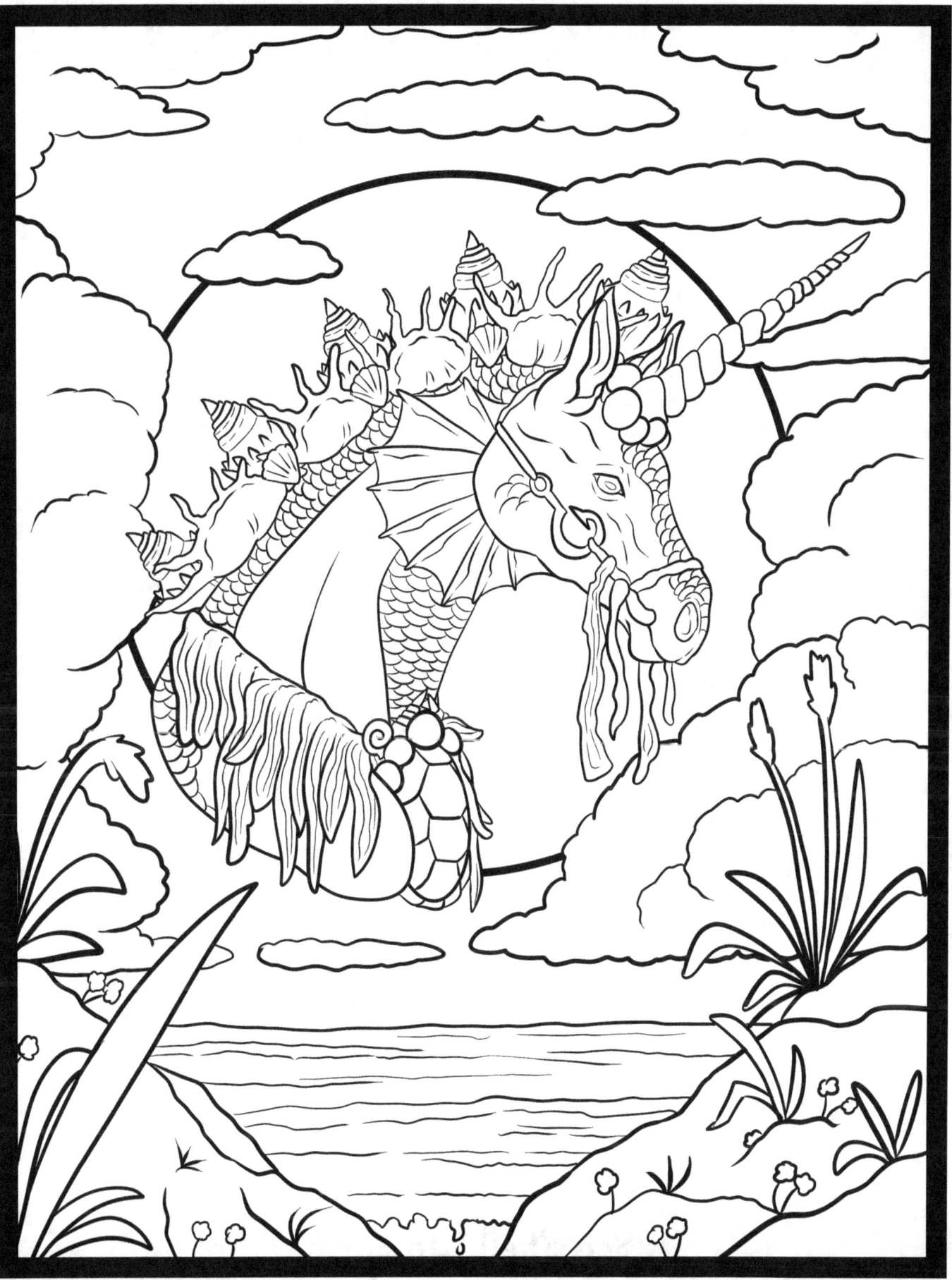

Sea Shell Unicorn

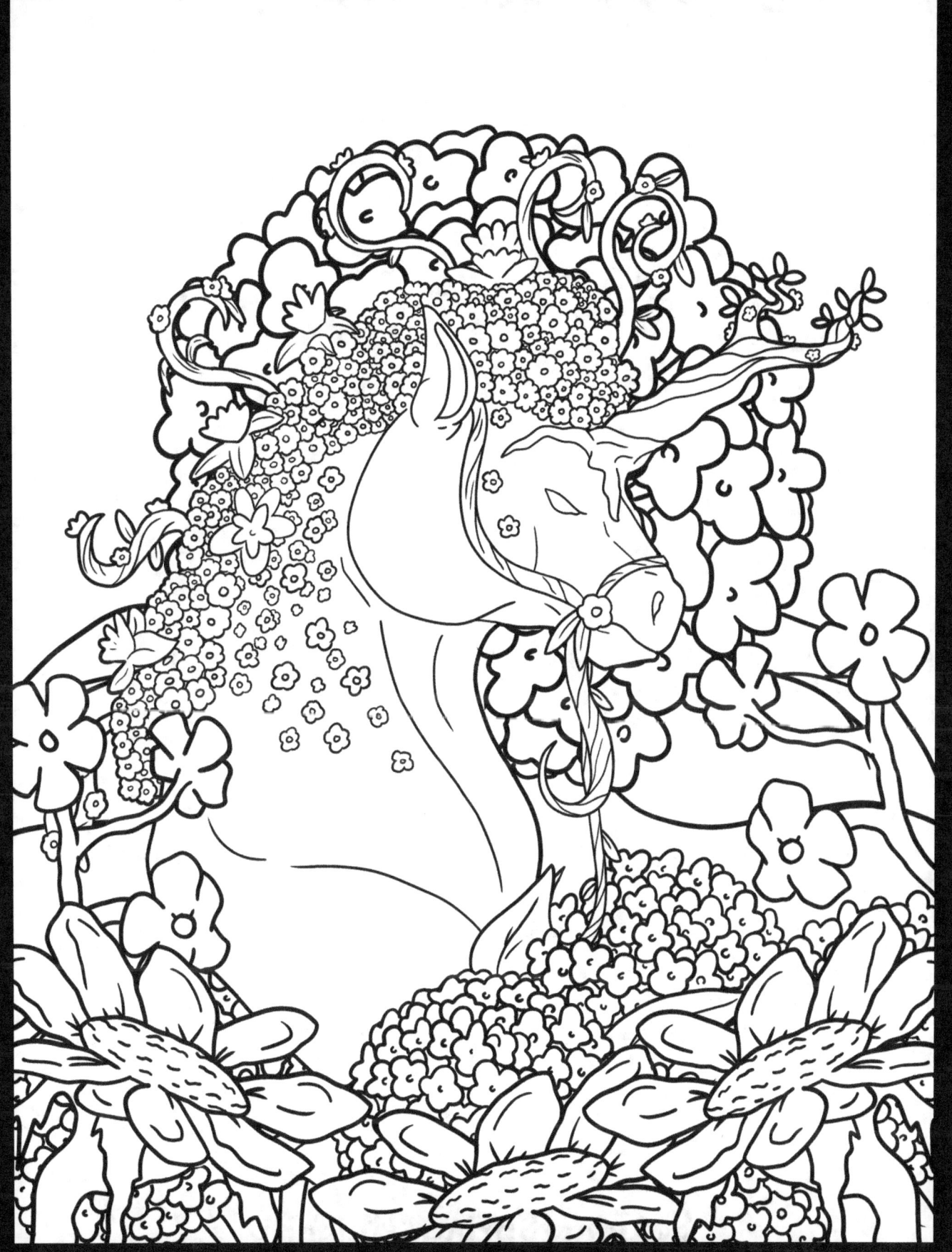

Seasons, Spring Unicorn

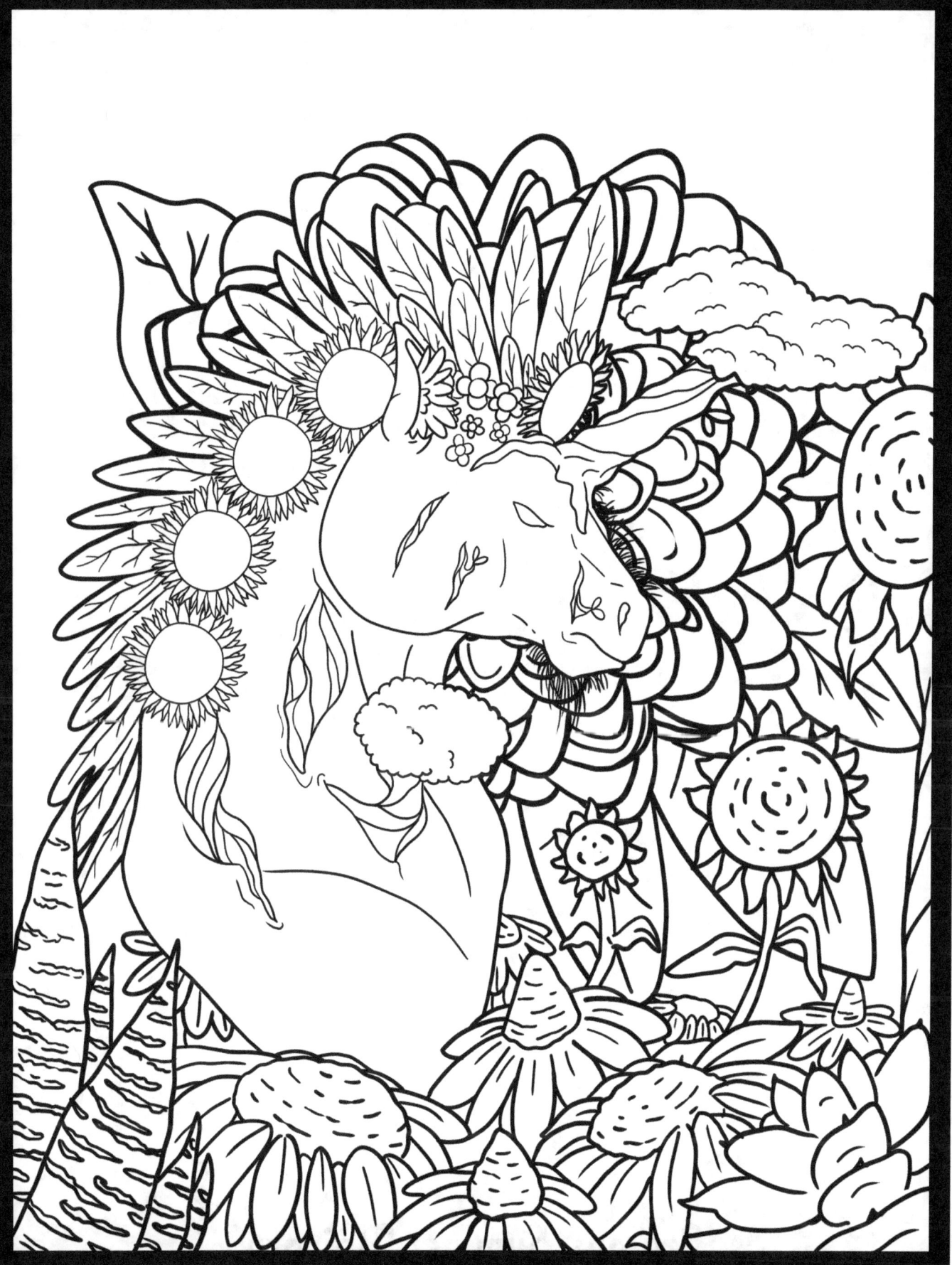

Seasons, Summer Unicorn

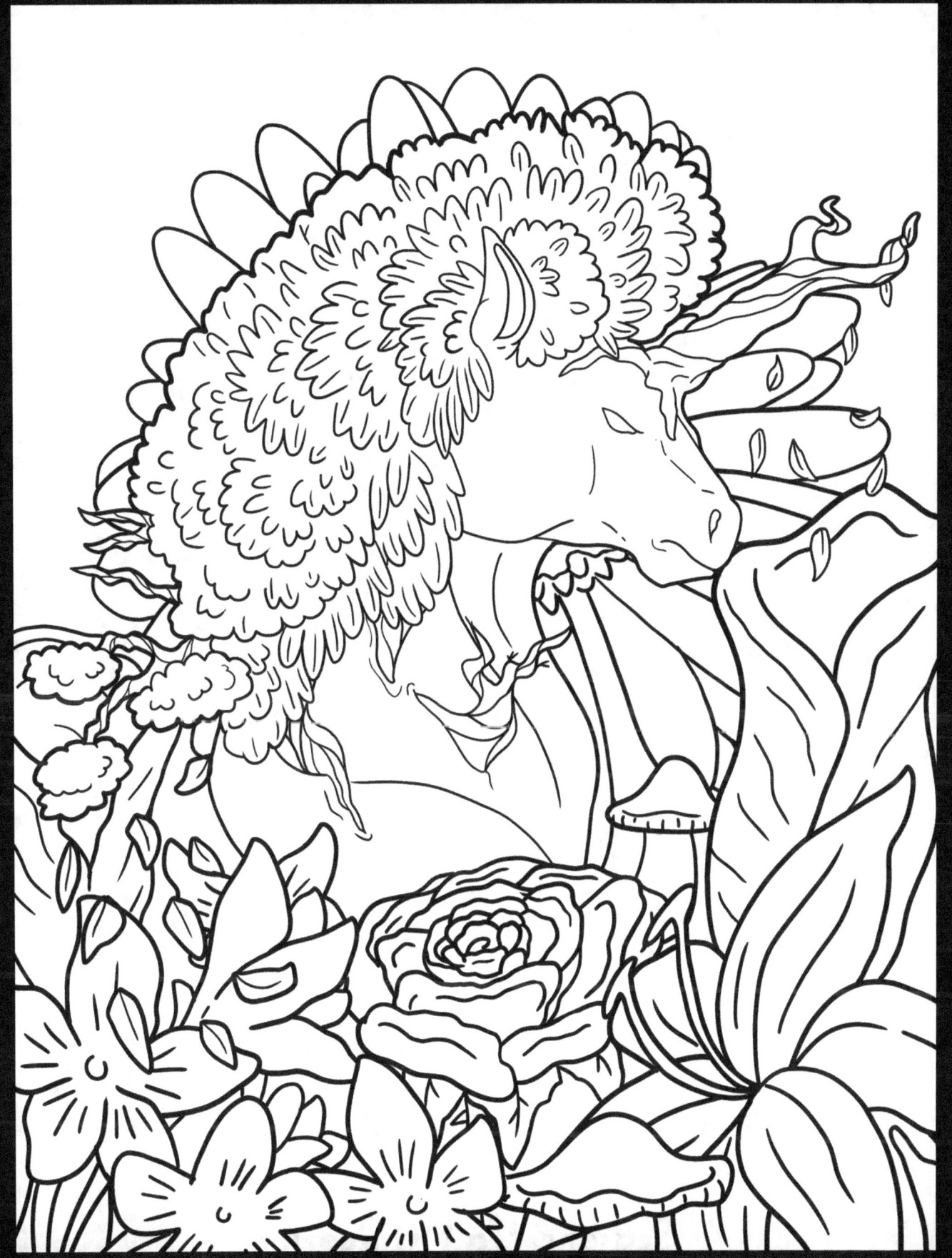

Seasons, Fall Unicorn

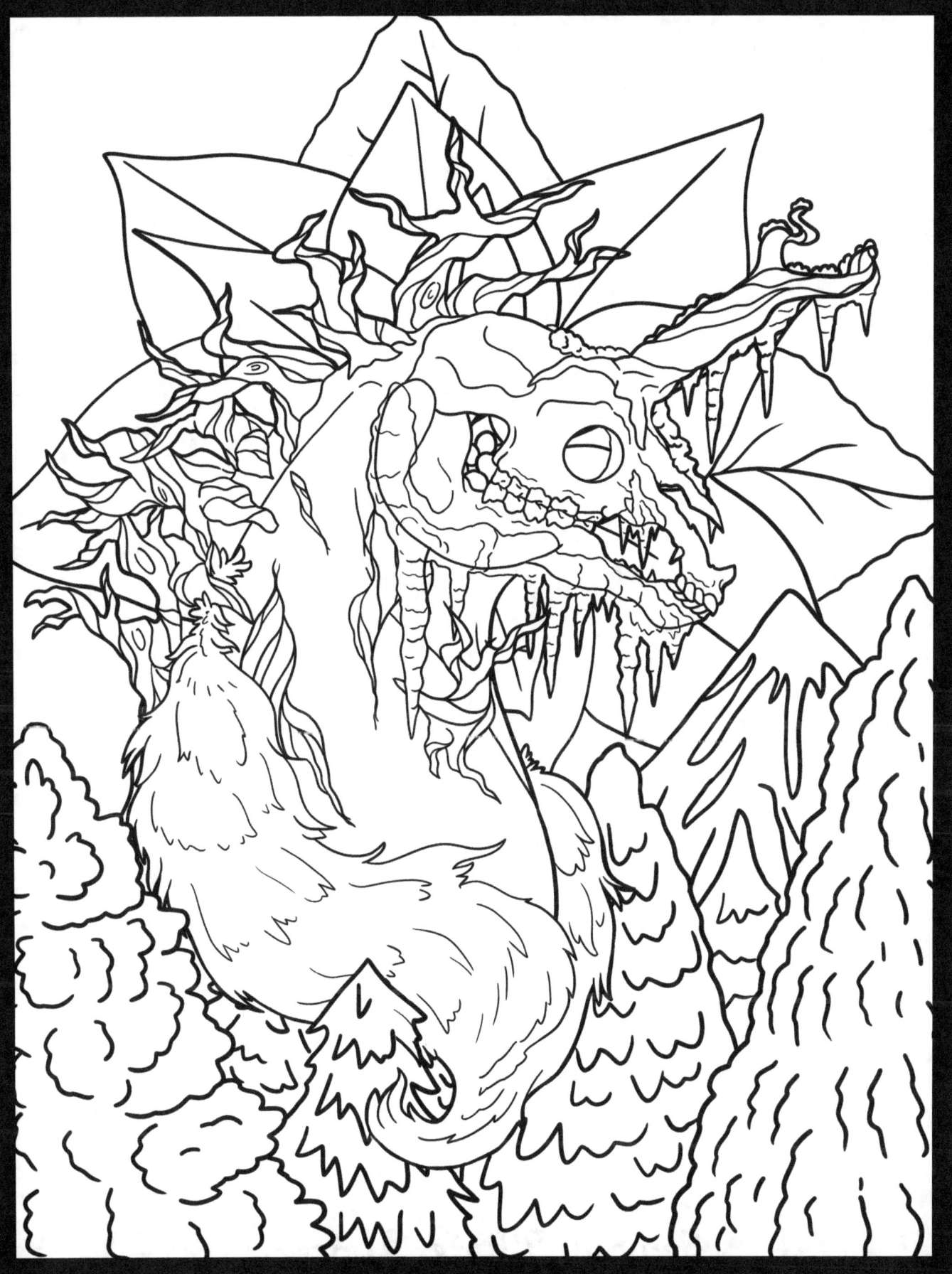

Seasons, Winter Unicorn

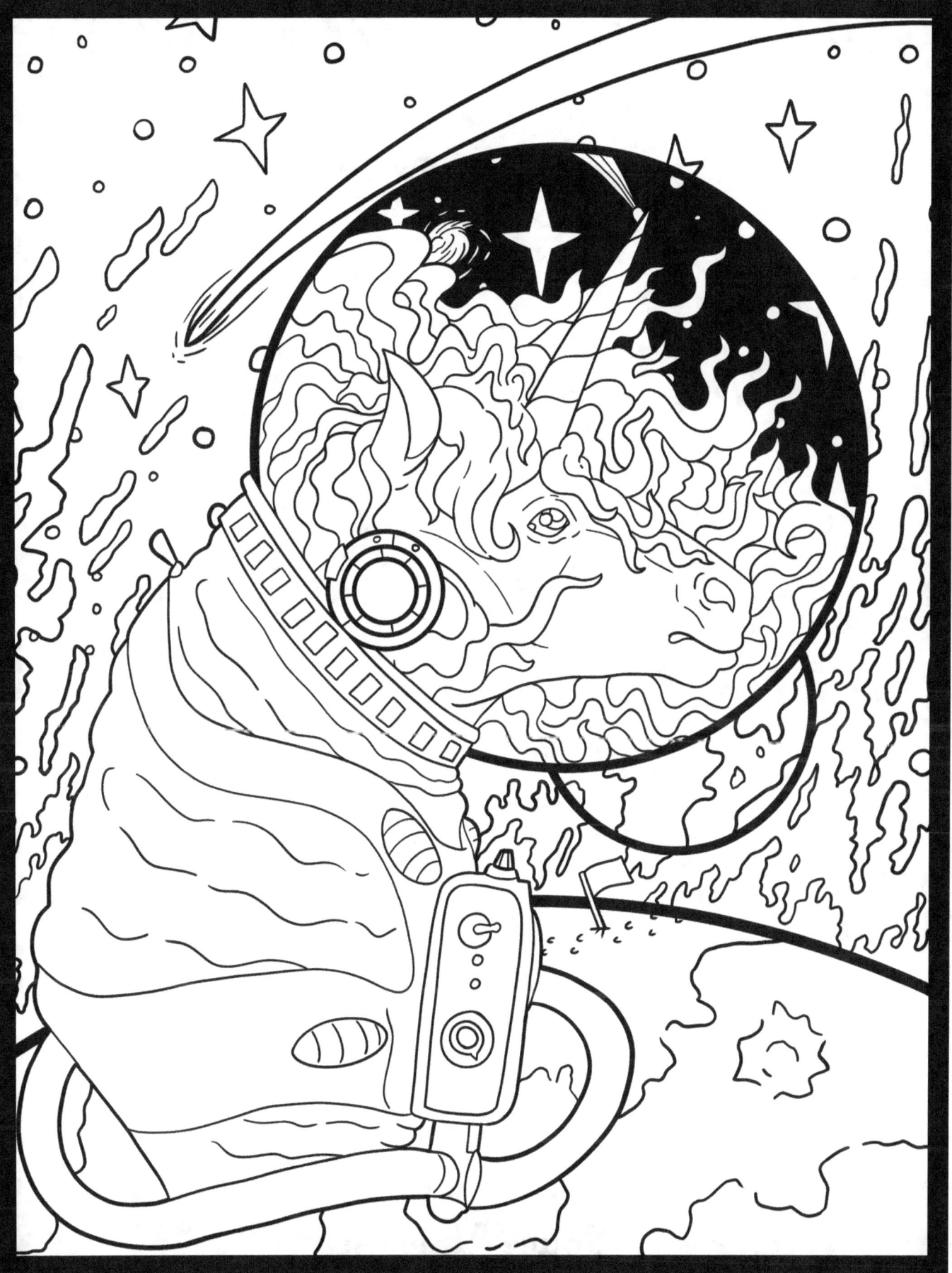

Space Unicorn

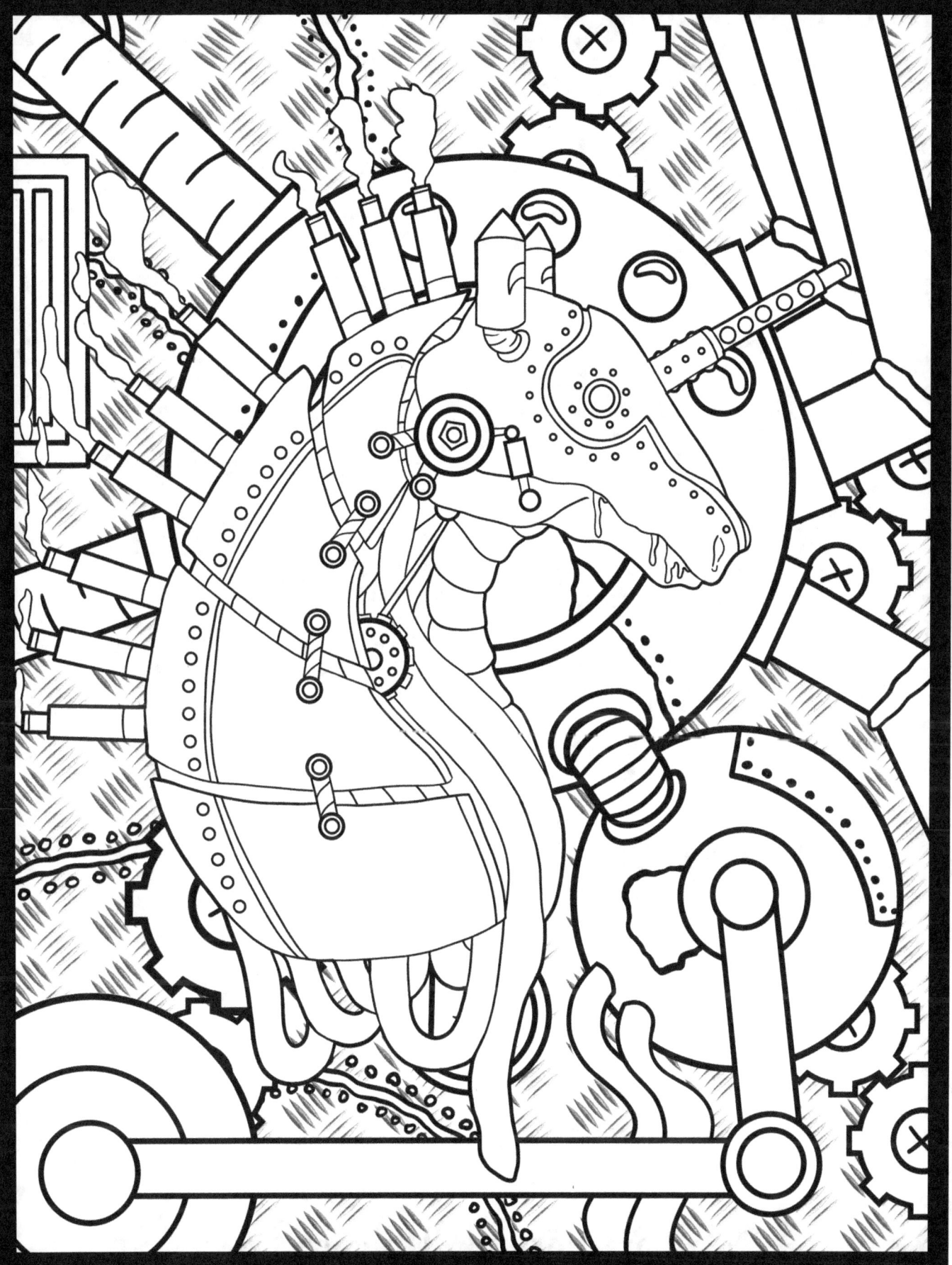

Steampunk Unicorn

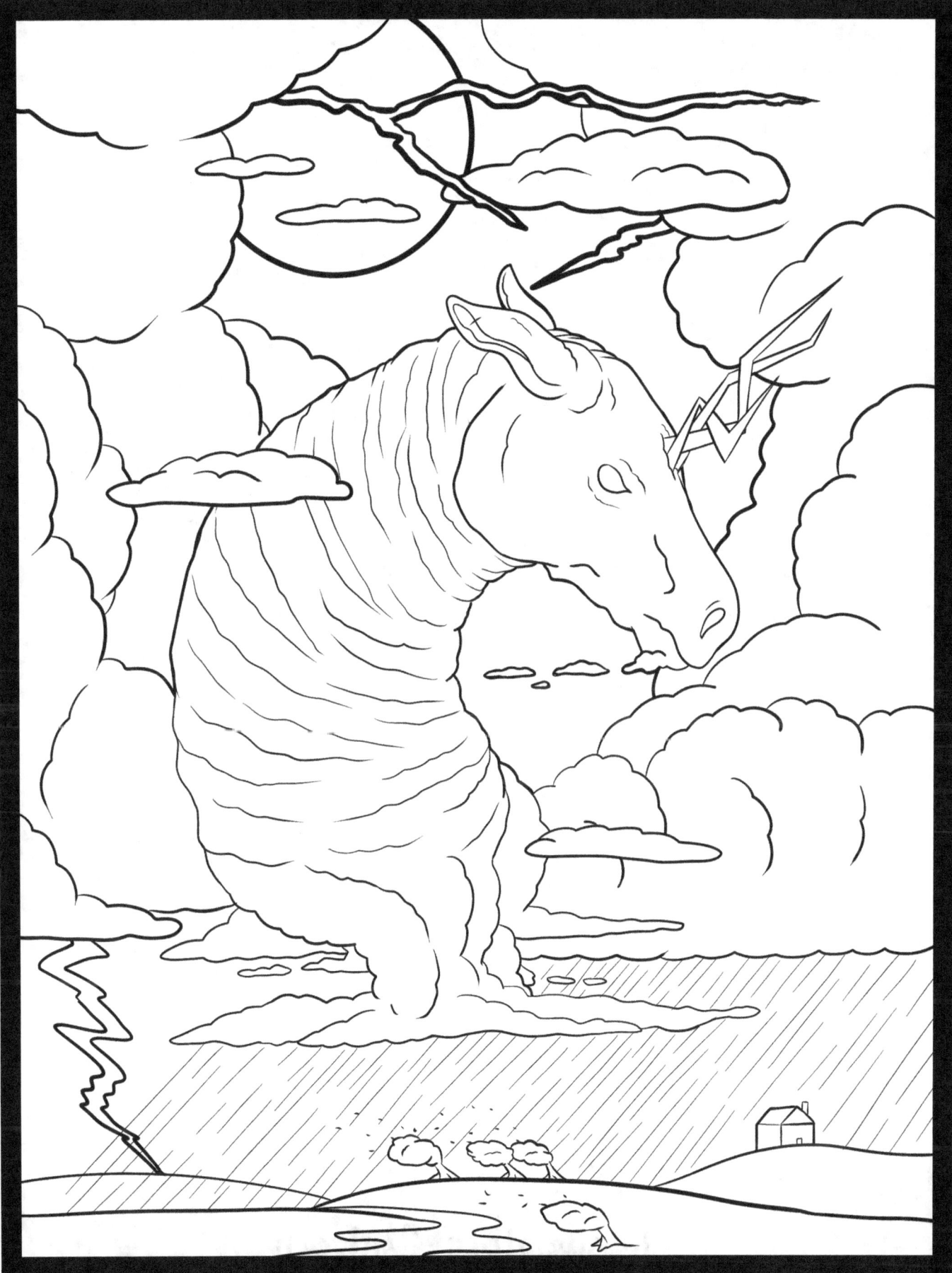

Thunderstorm Unicorn

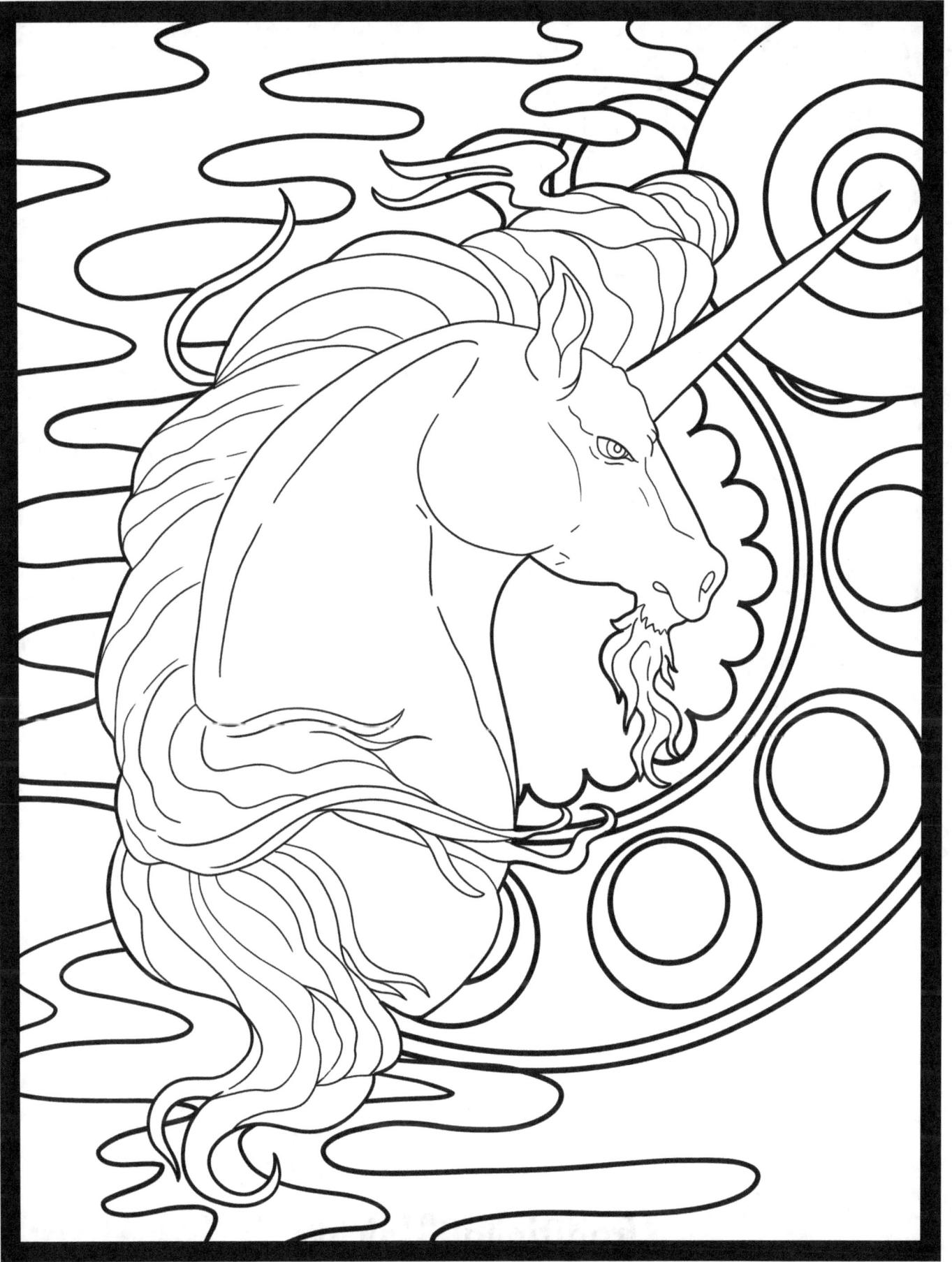

Traditional Unicorn

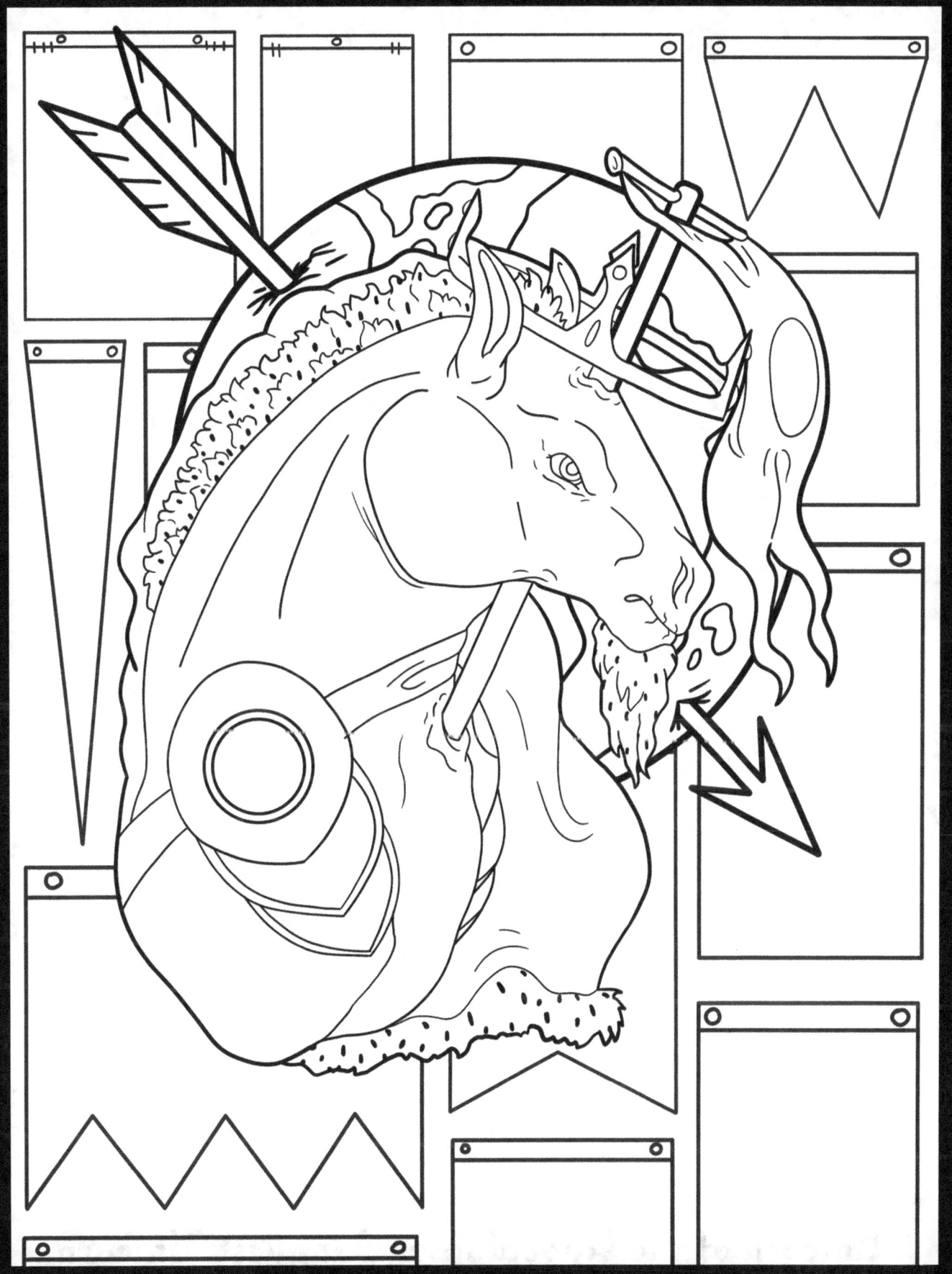

Unicorn of the Apocalypse: Conquest Unicorn

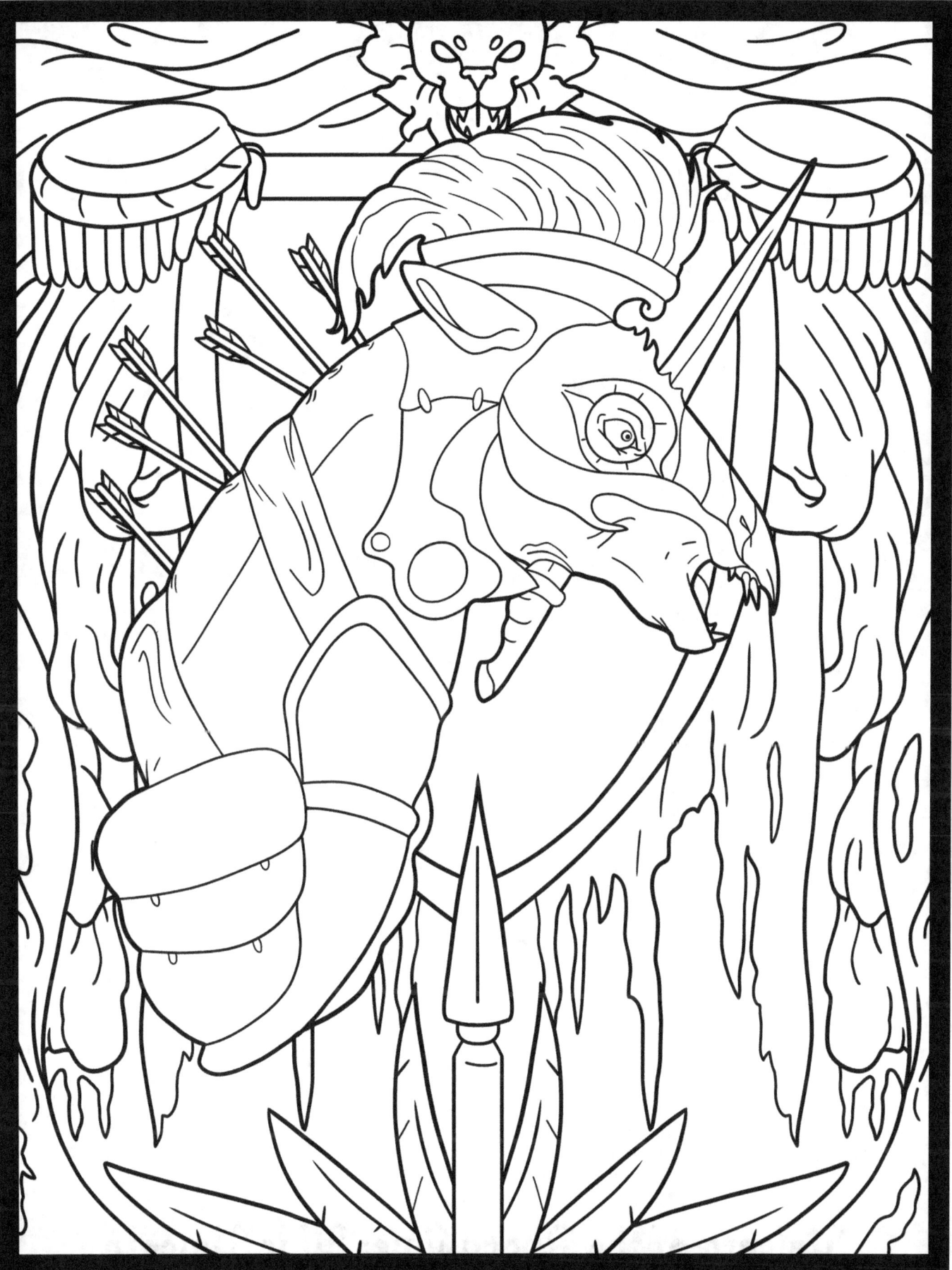

Unicorn of the Apocalypse: War Unicorn

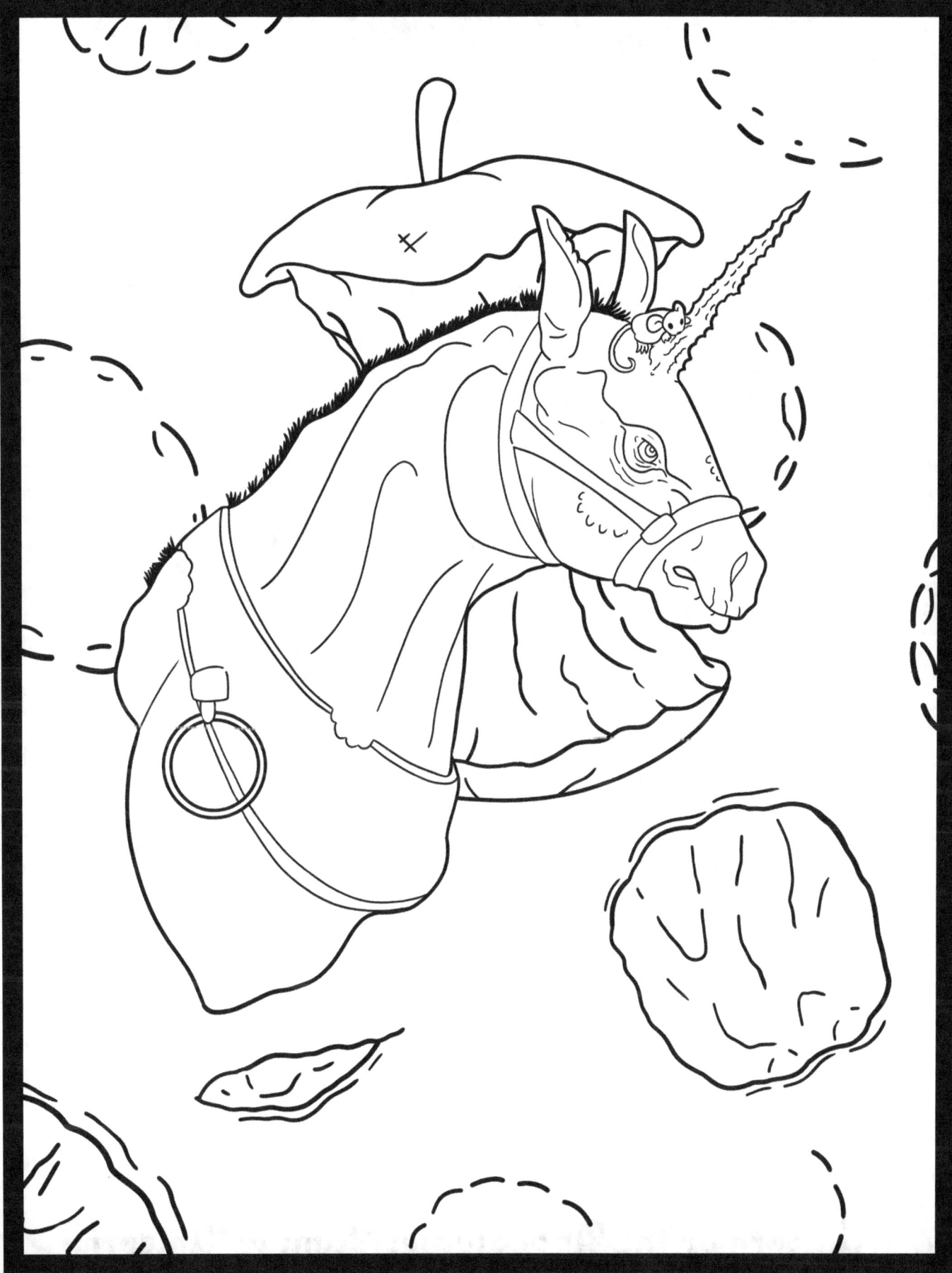

Unicorn of the Apocalypse: Famine Unicorn

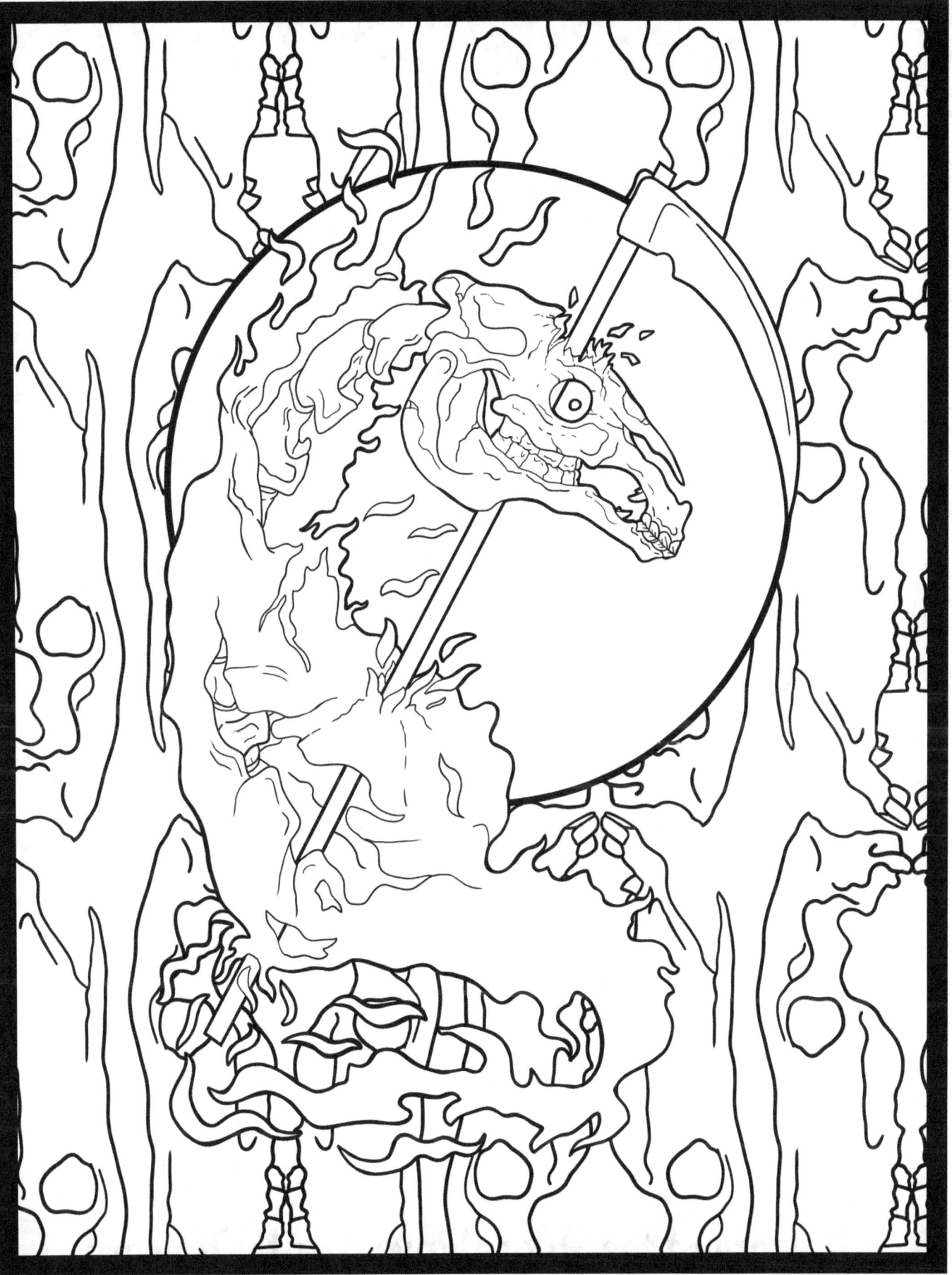

Unicorn of the Apocalypse: Death Unicorn